FIFTIES MOTOR RACING

THE **GP** SCENE
through the lens of Alan R. Smith

Best Wishes

Alan R. Smith

Foulis

Haynes

A **FOULIS** Motoring Book

First published 1990

© Alan R. Smith 1990

Published by:
Haynes Publishing Group
Sparkford, Nr Yeovil
Somerset BA22 7JJ, England

Haynes Publications Inc
861 Lawrence Drive, Newbury Park,
California 91320, USA

**British Library Cataloguing in
Publication Data**
Smith, Alan R.
    Fifties motor racing: the GP scene through the lens of
    Alan R. Smith.
    1. Formula 1 racing cars. Racing. Races: Grands Prix,
    history
    I. Title
    796.72

    ISBN 0-85429-747-2

Library of Congress Catalog Card Number
90-81736

Editor: Robin Read
Design: Rob Pattemore
Typeset in Times med roman 11/12pt
Printed in England by J. H. Haynes & Co. Ltd.

ACKNOWLEDGEMENTS

To supplement my own creaking memory of
motor-racing in the Fifties, I have tapped many
sources of information, including the helpful
recollections of various friends and acquain-
tances. I have been most grateful for their help.
I would particularly like to thank Roy Salvadori,
John Olliver and Graeme Simpson of Jarrotts,
and motor-racing journalist Eoin Young.

CONTENTS

To my wife Sheila, without whose practical help and enthusiastic encouragement this book would have never come to fruition.

INTRODUCTION

Name any sport under the sun, and it will have its band of enthusiasts – a band drawn from participants and spectators alike. Without such devotees, any sport would soon wither and die rather than flourish and breed legends to inspire and create nostalgia for future generations of avid followers.

The enthusiasm which the sport of motor-racing engenders is heightened by the fact that it has a dual personality, so to speak: driver and car inextricably linked from start to finish in victory or defeat.

There are, of course, the same twin elements in nostalgia for motor-racing of the past. Historic cars and drivers share their devotees.

It is the complete cocktail of a past era of motor-racing which tickles the palates of enthusiasts. The cars, the drivers, the action, are, of course, the main ingredients. 'Do you remember when Hawthorn's Ferrari . . . ?' 'they were working on Brabham's Cooper right up to . . .' 'Fangio's Mercedes' pit stop took only . . .' Such ingredients are spiked with glimpses of the circuits, team transporters, starting-grids, drivers chatting, pre-race preparations, and drivers' briefings, plus a host of other elements which combine to give the whole flavour of the time.

This book sets out to offer such a cocktail – mixed with the fresh ingredients of many hitherto unpublished photographs, and combined with a variety of personal recollections. These stem from photographing, watching and imbibing the excitement, spectacle, and atmosphere of the day.

Some people are born enthusiasts, others have enthusiasm thrust upon them. With regard to motor-racing, I came in the latter category, at least initially.

As a schoolboy in the mid-Thirties, I was given a box camera. After photographing friends, relatives, and anyone who would stand and emulate a latter-day terracotta soldier, I looked around for more exciting subjects. Aeroplanes had become my passion, and, living near Croydon Aerodrome, I took my camera down there. I quite enjoyed it, but I must have been imbued with a warlike streak, for I soon found that civil

aeroplanes did not really match up to my expectations. At the nearby RAF stations of Biggin Hill and Kenley there were fighter planes which were far more exciting to photograph, if I could get near enough – which I couldn't, most of the time!

One of my brothers, four years my senior, had recently left school, started working in the family business, and learned to drive. He managed to scrape enough together to buy a secondhand Two-plus-Two MG, and soon after took his girlfriend to a meeting at Brooklands. Their immediate enthusiasm was infectious, and they offered to take me along with them on a future occasion to see the racing. I jumped at the chance, because I thought it might be fun, and also because I knew that Brooklands Aerodrome was the home of Vickers Aircraft, then building RAF bombers.

The Brooklands Tunnel under the track provided a dramatic entrance to the motor-racing scene, particularly for first-timers. Greeted by the roar of cars passing one another at speed on the Outer Circuit banking, and seemingly within touching distance as one emerged into the paddock, the spectacle could be guaranteed to stir the imagination of the most blasé spectator. The paddock itself, with its evocative aroma of burning Castrol 'R', contained a wondrous selection of machinery to watch and photograph: Bentleys, ERAs, Rileys, Alfas, MGs, and Outer-Circuit giants, with a galaxy of famous drivers – Cobb, Mays, Howe, Bira and the rest . . .

The Brooklands Paddock possessed an added advantage: it was an amphitheatre enclosed within the outer circuit home banking, and provided a natural setting for a budding action photographer to practice high-speed 'panning'. My brother and I expended a great deal of film trying to capture cars at speed high on the banking, but usually a couple of smudges across the negative was all that our box cameras produced. On one memorable occasion, my brother did succeed in getting a passable shot of Cobb's Napier-Railton in action. I was furious that it wasn't mine!

In the latter half of the Thirties, the Germans, with their Mercedes and Auto-Union works teams, had brought a new concept to Grand Prix motor racing. Their cars, equipment, and highly efficient organisation, aided, of course, by a select band of top drivers, enabled them to quickly dominate Grand Prix racing, and become a legend in the space of a few years.

On the occasion of their first appearance on British soil at the Donington Grand Prix of 1937,

their effect on the British motor-racing public had been electrifying. So, when my brother offered to take me to Donington the following year to see the Germans, I needed no second bidding.

Impressions of that occasion are among my most treasured motor-racing memories, with no thrills barred. They include recollections of wandering round the Donington Paddock that golden autumn day, snapping away with our cameras at the Mercs and Auto-Unions as they were rolled off their transporters and warmed up. Or rubbing shoulders with our idols, Lang, von Brauchitsch, Nuvolari, and others. It is amazing to recall that a mere fifty spectators, or less, shared the paddock with us that morning – ah, halcyon days!

In the spring and early summer of 1939, ominous war clouds were gathering on the horizon. I continued to cycle down to Brooklands in my school holidays, and would surreptitiously photograph Hurricanes and Wellingtons on the aerodrome. When chased off, my friends and I would cycle on to watch, and probably photograph, race practice on the new Campbell Circuit.

My last motoring memory of that era, two days before war broke out, was going with my brother to fill up the 15-gallon slab tank of his TA MG – 'petrol may be in short supply' – we were broke for weeks!

In the absence of racing cars and real aeroplanes to photograph, I took to photographing my collection of model planes, strung up on cottons against the sky. My pictures were often unsharp, and I had no close-up lens on my box camera, but this must have added an air of realism, I suppose. The local chemist refused to develop and print my photos any more. 'You're not allowed to photograph planes in wartime, my lad. Next time, I'll send for the police!'

I was hopping mad, and decided I'd process my own photos, though I'd no idea how to do it. I'd just started work, so I saved up and bought chemicals and paper, a developing tank, and an ENSIGN POPULAR enlarger for under £10. I also bought my first real camera – a 16 on 120 ZEISS NETTAR, for £3.7.6! I was back to photographing friends and relations because of the defence regulations on photography, but unaccountably aeroplanes did sometimes appear on my negatives!

In 1940, my brother was called up for the army, and, sadly, later died a prisoner-of-war in Singapore. In 1942, I joined up as an RAF photographer. After my square-bashing, followed by 5 photographic training at the RAF No.1 School of Photography, Farnborough, I was posted to the Middle East, and spent the next 2½ years in the Mediterranean theatre of war. My working life seemed to be set in a succession of dark-rooms, varying from a castle in Malta to a caravan in Italy. However, whenever I could get into the air with a camera, I did so. This rein-forced my leaning towards action photography, particularly with large cameras. Talking of lean-ings reminds me that, after hostilities ceased, whilst leaning out of an open aircraft hatch to photograph Rome, I nearly dropped my camera, and myself on to the dome of St. Peter's!

In 1948, I returned to work in the family bus-iness. Motor sport was starting up again in a small way, and I took my fiancée to a hill climb at Falmer Park near Brighton.

Included in the programme I spied John Bol-ster driving his well-remembered Special 'Bloody Mary'. The sight of Bolster and car, plus a couple of ERAs, and the familiar figure of Earl Howe presiding over the scene, did much to rekindle the spark of enthusiasm for motor-racing within me.

To my shame, I failed to spot the potential of two contestants that day, namely R. Salvadori (Maserati), and S. Moss (Cooper-JAP) – clock-ing up an early victory!

I entered my MG TA for the Brighton Speed Trials. I certainly set no records, and recalling the almost completely bald state of tyres, it's amazing that I got past the scrutineers, but new tyres were like gold dust in those days! However, I did manage to get some shots of two of my old racing idols: Raymond Mays in his ERA R4D, and Siamese Prince 'B. Bira' with his beau-tiful 2.9 Maserati.

Hearing that there was to be a full-length Grand Prix motor race at a converted airfield in Northants, we set out to find this place, Sil-verstone. For some obscure reason, I had gone without a camera, so have no pictures of the main protagonists, Ascari and Villoresi, in their red 4CLT Maseratis, having it very much their own way. But they did keep swapping the lead to give the crowd some interest. I'd never heard of Ascari – maybe no one else here had at that time – but I did know the silver-haired Villoresi. I had last seen him 9 years before, sitting on his 3-litre Maserati in the paddock at Donington – complete with jet-black hair!

I'd always liked square format cameras, and bought a second-hand 6 x 6 cm. ZEISS IKOFLEX, perhaps not the ideal camera for action photography, but it was fitted with a 'frame' viewfinder, and had shutter speeds up to a 500th sec., which were useful attributes. Anyway, it was the best I could afford at the time.

Without a telephoto lens, the need to get a Press Pass was essential. I managed to obtain one for the 1949 British Grand Prix at Silverstone. It wasn't a track pass, but with a bit of bluff I made-do. It took a lot more time and persever-ance before I got regular track passes.

In common with most aspects of life in the immediate post-war period, motor sport was struggling against many odds to re-start and regain something of its pre-war position. Short-ages of materials of all kinds beset the would-be racing-car renovator or constructor. In Britain there was also the immense disadvantage of having lost both our major motor-racing cir-cuits at Brooklands and Donington. Airfield cir-cuits seemed but a very poor substitute, but it was Hobson's Choice.

On the Continent, with real road-racing on public roads, the streets were at least still there. One Continental motor-racing country quick to take up the cudgels again was Italy. With Ger-many's exclusion from international motor-racing, the major pre-war thorn in the Italians' side had gone and the Alfa-Romeo Tipo 158 Works team was quick to assert its supremacy.

In Britain, pre-war stalwarts including ERAs, Rileys, MGs, and 1930s Maseratis, etc., still made up much of the starting grid. But new Brit-ish car designs were gradually coming to fruition.

A new cheaper class of racing car had been evolved here, utilising 500 cc motor cycle engines. Led by a small constructor – Cooper, at Surbi-ton – these small cars were providing relatively inexpensive, but still exciting, racing for a wider range of competitors. Constructors such as HWM and Connaught, later to be joined by Cooper, were developing new 2-litre Formula Two cars. Up at Bourne, in Lincolnshire, that doyen of ERAs and Champion of British motor sport, Raymond Mays, was pressing ahead with the realisation of his great dream of a success-ful British Grand Prix contender. This was the 1½-litre V16 BRM, first demonstrated in public before the King and Queen at the 1950 Grand Prix d'Europe at Silverstone.

Sadly, events in the form of a change of the Grand Prix Formula soon dealt a great blow to this courageous project. However, the name BRM was to go on beside other British marques to enjoy successes in the years to come, which offset its early failures.

With the passage of time, the bleak British airfield circuits started to gather their own moss – if the pun may be excused! Silverstone and Goodwood etc., were acquiring their own identities and devotees.

Over the next ten years or so, motor sport shook itself free from the chains of war, and went on to regain and surpass its pre-war glory as a superbly exhilarating sport for contender and spectator alike.

This was a time of great change and great spectacle, as Ferrari snatched the mantle of glory from Alfa Romeo. In 1954-55 Mercedes made their dramatic but all-too-brief return to the sport, and soon Vanwall raised the name of a British Grand Prix team to the heights.

To pilot these cars to victory a new breed of driver took over the baton from great names of the past: Fangio, Ascari, Gonzales and their peers. From this country came some of the finest

drivers there had ever been: Moss, Hawthorn, Collins, Salvadori, Brooks and – from the Antipodes – Jack Brabham.

In the late Fifties, at the height of the Vanwall-Ferrari-Maserati struggle, the seemingly audacious victories of the diminutive Cooper-Climax heralded the future of Grand Prix car design changeover to rear-engine cars, thus bringing full circle a concept initiated by Ferdinand Porsche for Auto-Union 25 years before!

I hope that, however small the contribution, those who follow a sport in their thousands also may contribute a part of the whole. I was privileged to follow and record with my camera some of the many exciting aspects of a great motor-racing era. It was an experience I would not have missed for all the world.

In these pages I will share some of my most enjoyable memories with you, the reader.

FOREWORD

The 1950s were particularly exciting years for motor-racing – an era of great change, with new cars, new drivers and new concepts.

It was the time when British drivers started to make their mark in GP racing – winning many of these championship races, and in fact in 1958, when Mike Hawthorn won the championship, the first four places were taken by British drivers. It was also during this period that Coopers brought out their rear-engined F1 car, with which Jack Brabham won the World Championship in 1959; after which racing car constructors followed the Cooper example and designed and raced light-weight, rear-engined cars.

As a successful racing driver competing regularly in a wide variety of events, and being deeply involved in various aspects of the sport at that time, this evocative book strikes chords and brings back many happy memories of racing in the Fifties, tinged with sadness for the loss of some great personalities during this period.

I hope it may awaken similarly enjoyable nostalgic recollections for a variety of enthusiasts who revelled in those exhilarating racing days, as well as giving a glimpse of that era to the young followers of the present scene.

ROY SALVADORI
Monaco

I BOX CAMERA VIEW OF BROOKLANDS – AND DONINGTON

Brooklands was Mecca to most motor racing enthusiasts in the late Thirties. From the Test Hill to the new Campbell Circuit, from the Members' Clubhouse to the Byfleet Banking, Brooklands provided a kaleidoscope of interest, excitement and colour for devotees of the sport.

From Bentleys to ERAs, from 750 cc single-seater Austins to the many-litred giants of the Outer Circuit, the variety was infinite. Then there were the personalities to match, from those doyens of Brooklands such as Earl Howe and George Eyston to B. Bira with his impeccable blue-and-yellow équipe, managed by cousin Chula.

Nevertheless, Brooklands has always had its critics, being castigated as well as revered, some even claiming that its very existence was the reason why the law was never changed to allow racing on public roads in mainland Britain. This, and other arguments, will doubtless continue across the years. But nothing can alter the fact that, with all its faults, Brooklands holds a unique place in motor racing history.

The paddock at Donington Park in the Thirties was light-years removed in its simplicity from the sophistication and high-tec paddock scene of today. So it was when Mercedes and Auto Union came to Donington for the second year in 1938.

As a schoolboy box camera photographer, wandering round the paddock with my brother on that golden autumn morning, there seemed to be an atmosphere of unreality as we rubbed shoulders with our heroes, Nuvolari, von Brauchitsch, Lang, etc., clicking our shutters at the gleaming Mercs and Auto Unions as the mechanics drove them into the paddock. The shattering roar of revving engines reverberating across the peaceful parkland, coupled with the unforgettable fumes of exhausts burning exotic fuels leaving a taste on the tongue, etched indelible memories. Only about fifty other spectators shared the paddock with us that morning.

Von Brauchitsch of Mercedes shares a joke with Auto Union opponent Nuvolari, while the author eavesdrops!

8

Early 1936 Brooklands paddock scene with Thomson & Taylor mechanic Wuyts warming up ERA R10B in the foreground.

Box camera action shot of John Cobb's Napier-Railton at speed on the Home Banking. This formidable combination held the ultimate Brooklands Outer Circuit lap record at 143.44 mph.

*Christian Kautz, Auto-Union
driver, chats to one of his
mechanics across his car.*

*Sole Italian driver of an Italian
car, the debonair, then black-
haired Luigi Villoresi, strikes a
pose on his 3-litre Maserati –
but the backdrop is Mercedes!*

*W154 Mercedes. Note the
duster over the lower half of the
rad to exclude flying grit in the
paddock.*

II THE POSTWAR RESURGENCE OF MOTOR SPORT

In the immediate post-war period, hill climbs and sprints were types of events which were not too demanding for organisers in terms of finding suitable venues.

Falmer Park, near Brighton, offered a pleasant, if undramatic, hill climbing challenge.

In Brighton itself the annual one-kilometre Speed Trials, along the Madeira Drive, with an almost Continental backdrop, were revived.

John Bolster in action at Falmer Park with his famous sprint and hill climb Special 'Bloody Mary'. Bolster, a tremendous character, was later to make a name for himself as a motoring commentator and journalist.

At the Brighton Speed Trials in 1947 the enigmatic Bira, wearing tinted goggles and matching blue linen helmet and overalls, was driving his beautifully-prepared blue and yellow ex-Whitney Straight 2.9 Maserati. The sight of Bira, above all, brought so many nostalgic echoes flooding back to me of the glamour and excitement of pre-war motor-racing.

Earl Howe, 'father' of British motor racing, unmistakable with familiar cap and elegant cigarette holder.

An early appearance of Bob Gerard with his ERA. He was to become one of the most successful British competitors of the early Fifties, driving among other cars, beside his ERA, a Cooper Bristol and a Connaught.

III EARLY SILVERSTONE

1949 British Grand Prix

In its formative years, Silverstone was the cradle of truly competitive Grand Prix motor racing in Britain.

In sharp contrast to the Donington Grands Prix of 1937 and 1938, where there were virtually two races in one, as the ERAs and 'also rans' could not hope to compete seriously with the German teams, now all contestants in a British Grand Prix were expected to compete on equal terms. Of course, the capabilities of some participating cars were certainly not up to scratch for a full length Grand Prix!

Silverstone in those early days was a great melting pot where old and new met and did

battle. Veteran drivers such as Mays and Chiron mingled with up-and-coming youngsters like Moss and Collins. 4½-litre Lago-Talbots shared the paddock with new 500 cc Coopers – first-born of a stable destined to breed future Grand Prix winners.

Bob Gerard, looking more like an Oxford don than a racing driver, was one of the most successful British contestants in the late Forties and early Fifties. His successes included second in the 1949 British Grand Prix, driving his ERA. He later went on to drive Connaughts and Cooper Bristols, also very successfully.

Early days for a future master: Stirling Moss, Cooper-JAP, on the starting grid for the 500 cc. curtain-raiser. Father Alfred stands at the ready, spanner in hand, and useful rag in belt! Stirling won this race – just one of a variety of successes with the Cooper that year.

Reg Parnell, seen here with his 4CLT/48 San Remo Maserati, was one of the hard core of experienced British drivers who 'bridged' the war years, having started racing in the Thirties. He was to go on to be one of the most successful early post-war British drivers with a wide range of cars. (Right)

Louis Chiron (Lago-Talbot) chats to his mechanic. Although Chiron was past his peak, this Monagasque doyen of motor racing in the Thirties brought a certain ambience to the Silverstone racing scene.

Everyone mucks in. Bira rolls
along a newly-shod wheel for his
Maserati. Dapper as always, no
matter what he was doing, his
neat unflurried driving seemed to
reflect the same style.

4CLT/48 San Remo Maserati
cockpit. Note angled central
gear lever, and 4-spoked wood-
rimmed steering wheel.

Bira and Villoresi, 4CLT/48
Maseratis, play follow-my-leader
around the straw-bale chicane at
Club Corner, which was
scrapped for the following year,
1950. (Right)

One of the first Ferraris seen in this country was the 1½-litre supercharged Tipo 125. This car, painted pale grey, was brought over to Britain by Tony Vandervell, and driven by Raymond Mays, and Ken Richardson (who crashed it) – an inauspicious début for this famous marque!

This frontal shot of the inscrutable Bira in his Maserati clearly shows the famous White Mouse emblem on the front grille. Bira finished third in the Grand Prix. 19

Garlanded Baron de Graffenried, winner of the 1949 British Grand Prix, beside his Maserati.

Talbot-Lagos, which had been carried forward from a pre-war design, were a mainstay of racing in the late Forties and early Fifties. Naturally favoured by the French contingent of Chiron, Étancelin and Rosier, other drivers included Johnny Claes (Belgium), who had a number of successes with the marque, and Duncan Hamilton, who had one for a time. It was a big car that seemed to suit big personalities. This shot of the cockpit shows the large comfortable seat, sturdy four spoke steering wheel, and preselector gear change.

A great character among Talbot drivers was 'Phi-Phi' Étancelin, instantly recognisable with his back-to-front cap reminiscent of the pioneer days of motor racing. This picture of Étancelin in action also gives some idea of the sheer bulk of the Lago-Talbot.

The Lago-Talbot 6-cylinder 4½-litre unblown engine, cast in light alloy, with inclined over-head valves operated by push rods from twin, high mounted camshafts. Note the 3 large sidedraught Zenith carburettors, of this earlier car and the forward-facing air intake. These were not by any means the fastest of cars, but nor were they the thirstiest either. This was how Talbot could occasionally trounce its 1½-litre blown fuel-guzzling rivals!

21

The Drivers

Dress tended to be pretty informal for racing in those days – maybe a pair of grey flannel bags (slacks to this generation): perhaps an old shirt and sweater, or, if you had some overalls to wear, they'd do fine.

Headgear was varied, and footwear likewise. Some drivers favoured a comfortable old pair of tennis or golf shoes – anyway, clothes rationing was still in force for the British, so race organisers needed to be flexible. Oh yes: drivers did need a pair of goggles or a visor. If it were the former, they may well have been war surplus, purchased for a few shillings, and had probably seen action only a few years previously with an RAF bomber or fighter pilot.

Among the drivers present at this briefing are Ken Richardson, Bira, George Abecassis, John Heath, and Reg Parnell (seen just behind Bob Gerard, who's busy blowing his nose!)

Earl Howe, Steward of the meeting, is briefing the drivers. Very few Englishmen could lay claim to being so deeply involved in motor-racing for such a long period as Howe.

From being one of the most eminent British racing drivers of pre-war days, he progressed after the war to presiding, as a most respected and knowledgeable senior official, over more British race meetings than I'd care to count. For many years, he was also the British representative on the Sporting Committee of the FIA (Féderation Internationale des Automobiles).

Young 500cc drivers Moss and Collins watching the Grand Prix. How many of those who stood in the crowd beside them had any inkling that within a few years these two young men would be rated among the world's top Grand Prix drivers?

The First Daily Express International Trophy

When the Daily Express staged the first of these meetings at Silverstone in 1949, they set a standard for prestigious, non- championship major races.

Having changed horses from Maserati to the new Ferrari, Ascari (hands on hips) stands beside team-mate Villoresi's car at the start of Heat Two.

Starting grid, International Trophy Final. The Maseratis of Farina (30) and Parnell shared the front line of the grid with Ascari's Ferrari. Here, Farina's mechanic stands with starting handle at the ready. In those days the start line and Motor bridge, as seen here, were just above Abbey Curve.

Farina, edging ahead of Parnell, was to finish second, splitting the two works Ferraris. Ascari, the winner, has already gone. Villoresi is beyond Parnell's right shoulder.

The Dawn Road to Silverstone

In the early Fifties the traffic problems created by a crowd of around 100,000 converging on Silverstone was a new and daunting experience for race organisers, public and police alike. Attendances at pre-war race meetings, even the Donington Grands Prix, had been but a fraction of the numbers now coming to a major race.

Thus the bi-annual pilgrimage to the Northants circuit for the Daily Express International Trophy and the British Grand Prix assumed in the mind of the enthusiast the proportions of an expedition. How to beat the traffic and get there in time: that was the problem.

From households all over the country long before dawn race enthusiasts would be tumbling out of bed to grab a quick breakfast and get on the road fast to try and beat those jams. My household was no exception. To this day several friends still bear the scars, mental at least, of my ruthless 'get-'em-up' methods.

Coming into Silverstone via Aylesbury we reckoned that we must get through Buckingham by 07.30 – 15 minutes later, and you could miss the start. On the other hand, the sense of achievement engendered as one drove on to the circuit with time in hand seemed akin to breasting the final ridge of the Eiger!

The crowds and traffic today are probably considerably bigger still, but the fun of those days is hard to match.

Royal Grand Prix d'Europe

When the 1950 British Grand Prix was designated Grand Prix d'Europe *for that year, it was honoured by the presence of King George VI and Queen Elizabeth, accompanied by the young Princess Margaret.*

Here the Royal party are seen watching the race from one of the Royal viewing platforms specially erected at various vantage points. Included in the Royal party were Earl Mountbatten – talking to Earl Howe – and Countess Mountbatten, extreme left.

But there was no hope in those days of cheering a British winner home, car or driver.

Before the Grand Prix, Raymond Mays made a brief demonstration run in the new V16 BRM. It looked and sounded wonderful, but everyone, including the Royal visitors, no doubt, was so disappointed that they could not see it competing.

In a race dominated by foreign cars in the form of the Alfa Romeo team, there was some patriotic interest in that Reg Parnell had been given a place in an Italian Works car that day.

The Alfas

If there is one car universally revered in the motor racing world, the mere mention of which brings mist to the eyes of the true enthusiast, it must surely be the Alfa Romeo Tipo 158 and its ultimate version, the 159.

Conceived in the late Thirties in an attempt to dominate voiturette racing, its early history, which included defeat by the 'secret' 1½-litre Mercedes at Tripoli in 1939, gave no hint of the remarkable string of successes in store for the 158 when it graduated to Grand Prix status after the war.

The impressive line up of the dominant Alfa Romeos prior to the race. The background illustrates the original tubular scaffolding pits situated between Abbey Curve and Woodcote Corner prior to 1952. For this august occasion the wooden pit counters were well-bedecked with an abundance of bunting – probably war victory parade surplus! However, someone did manage to find some Italian flags to fly above the pits of the almost certain winners!

A mechanic unloading an Alfa from its transporter. He is clearly concentrating on positioning the car, but it looks as if he needs to judge his own head clearance to a nicety!

Its track record is truly formidable: 45 Firsts out of 54 races: 11 wins in 11 races (1950 season): 2 Drivers' World Championships (Farina 1950 and Fangio 1951).

But, as if that were not enough, it was also probably the most sensuously beautiful racing car of all time to watch, even to hear, and certainly to photograph!

Dr Guiseppe Farina, initiator of the relaxed sit-back straight-arm driving technique, seen in action at Silverstone. He led the Alfas of Fagioli and Parnell home to a 1-2-3 victory – Fangio having dropped out with an oil leak.

That year, Farina went on to win the newly-instituted Drivers' Championship, thus becoming the first-ever World Champion Driver.

Photographers please note: when panning to photograph cars in action at these early Fifties race meetings, there was always a chance that one of the intermittent straw bales defining the inside of the corner would block a vital part of the car at the critical moment of exposure!

Straight Eight Par Excellence. An Alfa team mechanic changing plugs on one of the beautifully-prepared 158s (1.5 litres, 8 cylinders). Prominent in the picture is the massive 'ear trumpet' air intake to the carburettor above the first stage blower.

IV ACTION ON THE BREMGARTEN

The Swiss Grand Prix 1951

In 1951 I made plans to photograph my first Continental race. I had always wanted to go to the Swiss Grand Prix, run on the lovely wooded Bremgarten Circuit, situated on the outskirts of Berne.

Of course, I needed a photographer's track pass: that was the rub, so I wrote to the organisers, the Swiss Automobile Club, requesting one.

In the absence of any credentials to back up my request, I said that I intended to write a book on motor racing – it was a little premature – nearly forty years, in fact! However, back came a most courteous reply, saying that they assumed I must be 'very experienced at this sort of thing', and they would be pleased to accede to my request.

Once I arrived in Berne, I was anxious to get

Spectators sitting in the wooden stands opposite really did get a cracking view of the proceedings. Here, during the first afternoon's practice session, No. 2, Johnny Claes, Lago-Talbot, is seen moving out past the Alfa pits.

some pictures of the first practice session. Getting out to the Bremgarten was simplicity itself – just a short tram ride from the city centre. As I alighted near the circuit, I heard a throaty rumble, and Villoresi, wearing a natty sports jacket over his overalls, drove casually by at the wheel of a $4\frac{1}{2}$-litre Grand Prix Ferrari. I liked this introduction to Continental motor racing!

Practice

The attractions of the racing circuit at Berne were considerable. To me, partially-wooded circuits have a magic quality of their own, which I had first seen at pre-war Donington. I found that the Bremgarten also possessed that certain magic in full measure. To follow contestants by ear, yet out of sight, on their high-speed progression through the soundbox of the forest could be tantalising in the extreme. The crescendo and diminuendo of sound as drivers changed up and down was guaranteed to get spectators' adrenalin flowing long before the cars spewed out of the woods into full view.

The pits were situated just past the start area on a very fast right-hander, and were set back in a little lay-by. That section of the course was surfaced with wooden setts, which required great respect in the wet.

The pits themselves were built of stout seasoned Alpine timbers, as used in Swiss chalets. 31

Sanesi, Alfa's chief tester and reserve driver, puts a car through its paces. This model is fitted with the larger side fuel tanks.

The 4½-litre Ferrari was a beast of considerable bulk and size, but, like people, racing cars often have a 'better side' – at least where the camera is concerned! I am rather fond of this profile of the Ferrari, enhanced by the relaxed yet masterful attitude of driver Villoresi, as he accelerates through the long curving 'straight' towards the Bremgarten pits.

The Drivers

These pictures of drivers chatting with one another give glimpses of the relaxed and uncrowded atmosphere of this age of racing, both at practice sessions and even on race day.

Looking a bit like naughty schoolboys, Gonzalez and Fangio in a light-hearted mood. Fellow countrymen and old pals, they ofttimes raced together in the first half of the Fifties, sometimes as team-mates, sometimes in opposition to one another. Gonzalez' ebullient personality was in sharp contrast to the ever-calm Fangio.

At Berne, whilst Fangio was No.1 driver for Alfa-Romeo, Gonzalez had to be content with a rather slow Lago-Talbot, which packed up after ten laps. But Gonzalez' fortunes were soon to change, as we shall see later.

33

Old contemporaries Farina and Étancelin converse together. Both very experienced drivers, their knowledge of Grand Prix racing stretched back many years. Étancelin started racing in the early Thirties, and Farina had been an Alfa Corse Works driver, and twice Italian Champion in the late Thirties.

The young curly-haired Moss in earnest conversation with fellow-driver George Abecassis and the latter's partner John Heath (centre). HWM sometimes filled the role of giant-killer, especially in the hands of Moss, who 'shook' various Continentals driving much more powerful Works cars.

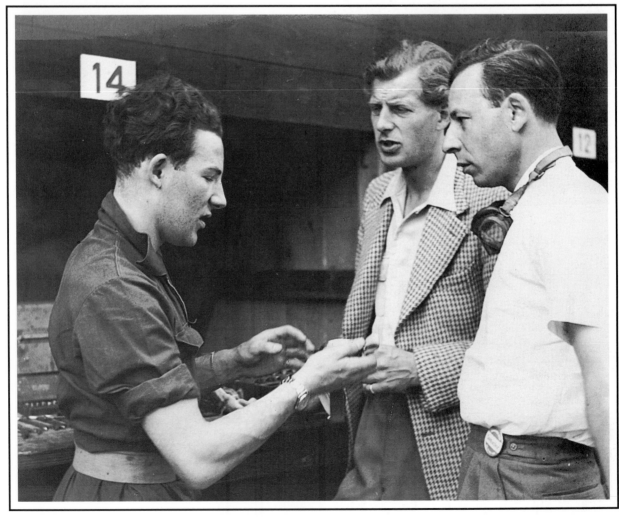

Cockpit Comparisons

4½-litre Ferrari, Large rev counter on right of dashboard, other instruments grouped two and two. Bulky prop shaft casing. Mirrors external to cockpit. Horse insignia on central wheel boss.

158 Alfa. Rev counter on left of dashboard, other instruments grouped three and one. Slim prop shaft casing. Mirrors internal to reduce wind resistance. Alfa Cloverleaf insignia on scuttle, and St. Christopher emblem central on dashboard with all Alfas.

Race Day

In contrast to the pleasant weather conditions prevailing during practice, race day was dull and wet, with a fine drizzle at the start, which increased to a good old Swiss soaking as the race progressed.

My admiration for the skill of drivers who could race Grand Prix cars in such conditions knew no bounds. There were casualties – Moss, HWM, had the added trauma of a shattered windscreen to cope with, and Villoresi ran out of road.

This was my first experience of photographing in the wet. As the rain increased, I was mainly concerned for my camera, especially keeping spots off the lens. To start with, I tried bending forward to shield my camera, then resorted to draping a somewhat damp handkerchief over the camera when not actually shooting. It was crude, but seemed to work.

From cursing the rain for its discomfort and inconvenience, I quickly came to appreciate and enjoy the unique atmosphere which the car reflections on the rain-soaked road, and spray from the wheels, create in an action picture. From then on, if I could not photograph in sunshine, I hoped it would pour!

Fangio about to take his Alfa out for practice. Here he wears the linen helmet, so long favoured by drivers.

Race day. Fangio (right) and Farina, before the start, wearing Pirelli waterproof smocks – maybe the first sign of drivers uniforms – plus a spot of advertising! For these conditions they favoured British-style racing helmets and visors. However, Farina also had a pair of goggles round his neck, just in case, but not so Fangio!

Swiss driver De Graffenried's Alfa. Note the huge ribbed brake drums, almost as big as the wheels! Also on view are the splash guards introduced by Alfas after the 'downpour' International Trophy at Silverstone two weeks earlier.

Ferrari newcomer Taruffi (44) shares the second row of the grid with team-mate Ascari.

Well-stocked with tyres. Louis Rosier, Talbot, comes prepared!

The Start. The Alfas of Fangio and Farina lead Villoresi's Ferrari ahead of the pack.

Foresthaus Corner in the pouring rain. Fangio, race leader, about to lap Claes' Talbot and Abecassis' HWM. Note the treacherous surface of the rain-soaked setts.

This picture of Villoresi in the wet shows a very different aspect of car and driver from the 'dry' practice profile.

A few laps later, Ascari skidded into the hedge. Both Ascari and Villoresi were out of luck that day, but team-mate Taruffi came in second, splitting the four Alfas, to demonstrate that Enzo Ferrari was snapping at the heels of his erstwhile employers in earnest!

Fangio, the winner, shows how to corner at 130 mph in the wet and still look relaxed! His win at Berne set him on the road to claiming the 1951 Drivers' World Championship – the first of five such victories.

V ALFA VERSUS FERRARI

The British Grand Prix 1951

This race, at least on paper, had mouth-watering possibilities, for not only was it to be a vital round in the supercharged 1½-litre Alfa versus 4½-litre 'unblown' Ferrari contest, but there was the additional prospect of two V16 BRMs competing in a Grand Prix for the first time. British hopes, even if somewhat unrealistic, were naturally running high.

The Ferrari Works cars undergo final adjustments in the paddock.

The Italian Connection. Farina (right) sits on a wheel of his Alfa having a relaxed pre-race chat with friends from the opposing Ferrari team, Ascari and Villoresi.

Unforeseen Development! On the start line, Farina climbs into his car, and Alfa mechanics stand at the ready with the starter motor as the five-minute warning sounds.

I had good cause to remember those next five minutes. This shot was the last on a roll, and I needed to change a film quickly. Now, rushing round to photograph a Grand Prix can be thirsty work, so to slake my thirst I had popped a couple of cartons of orangeade (purchased from the local cinema) into my camera bag – an ex-army gasmask haversack. Imagine my consternation when, reaching into the bag for a fresh film, my fingers encountered ten rolls of film sloshing around in a sea of orange! My heart sank. They'd be ruined!

But the devil's luck was on my side: the liquid had not yet seeped through the film cartons, and I was able to rescue the precious contents before they 'drowned'. In future I would go thirsty to work!

43

Parnell's BRM accelerating
away from the start line, in
pursuit of the already-gone Alfas
and Ferraris. Parnell finished
fifth, and team-mate Walker
seventh – valiant efforts after
enduring painful burning in the
overheating cockpits.

Gonzalez, in no mood to trifle, en route to trouncing the Alfas at last – for Ferrari. Even Fangio could do nothing to stop his victory. It was reported that the tough Enzo Ferrari expressed an element of sadness tingeing this victory over his erstwhile employers. This was also a victory for the large unblown engine over the smaller supercharged machine.

VI THE V16 BRM

The history of motor racing has its fair sprinkling of failure stories. However, among them some certainly brought added drama and colour to the sport of the day – none more so than the V16 BRM!

Was there ever a car which caused such frus-

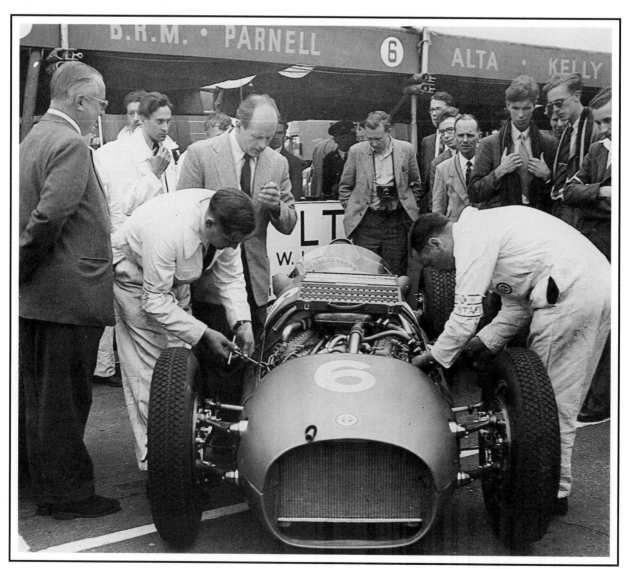

trations – which raised hopes so high, or dashed them so low – which was to bring forth such blistering comments from the distinguished drivers who handled it: Moss, Fangio, Parnell and Gonzalez?

This brainchild, this dream-to-come-true, of Raymond Mays and designer Peter Berthon, was more than that. In many respects it crystallized the longing of the British racing public for a car which, hopefully, at long last would wrest Grand Prix honours from the Continentals and give Britain a car to shout about. Sadly, this was not to be.

The V16 was a complex design, lacking the sort of consistent backing and experienced management necessary to develop and race such

Close-up of plug-change and the complex BRM 'plumbing'.

The stark BRM cockpit. Note unusual 'compass' type rev counter.

At the British Grand Prix, 1951 Parnell's BRM gets a pre-race plug-change, watched over by designer Peter Berthon and, on the left, Tony Vandervell, who was a considerable backer of the project at this time.

a car. There was also an unforeseen major factor against it, in that time was not on its side.

With great pressure on the BRM to show what it could do, it made a brief demonstration appearance prior to the 1950 Grand Prix d'Europe in the hands of Raymond Mays before the King and Queen.

Pressures and problems were to grow apace for the team over the next year, and it was against this uncertain background that two cars were entered for Reg Parnell and Peter Walker to face the proven strength of Alfa and Ferrari at the 1951 British Grand Prix.

All BRM's well-wishers hoped against hope that the cars could at least dent the Italian opposition, but these were vain dreams. It was, in retrospect, the swan song of BRM as a Grand Prix contender. A few months later Alfas retired, and by the next year, with little prospect of the British cars putting up serious opposition to Fer-

rari, race organisers switched to Formula Two, which became the *de facto* Grand Prix Formula for the next two years.

All this was a great blow to British expectations. Industrialist Alfred Owen and his organisation took over the ailing BRM team, but it was too late to put the clock back. The only events now open to BRM were Formula Libre races.

However, on the credit side, these races did provide considerable spectacle at many meetings over the next few years. Driven by top drivers such as Fangio, Parnell, Gonzalez, etc., they gave a wishful inkling of what might have been if the venture had succeeded.

Whatever the many failings of the V16, it could always be guaranteed to bring the crowds running, and cameras shooting. Everyone recognised the distinctive ear-blasting wail heralding its approach, and even at rest in the paddock no one would pass a V16 without a glance!

All eyes on Ascari as he tries the BRM wheel under the watchful gaze of its creator, Raymond Mays. Unlike Fangio and Gonzalez, Ascari never actually drove the BRM.

BRM's 'rescuer', Alfred Owen, shakes hands with Fangio before the start of the Formula Libre race at the 1952 British GP meeting.

Ken Wharton demonstrates how to 'handle the brute' on a rain-soaked track at Boreham in 1952. Note handkerchief in mouth, a handy emergency windscreen wiper!

Making a great show for spectators and photographers alike, with bags of tyre smoke, Gonzalez' and Parnell's BRMs beat Farina's Thinwall Special off the line at the 1952 Goodwood September Meeting.

51

That day, Raymond Mays shared a brief moment of glory with drivers Gonzalez, Parnell and Ken Wharton, seen here quaffing from the Winner's Cup.

In the early Fifties, industrialist Tony Vandervell, manufacturer of Thinwall bearings, who was a motor-racing enthusiast and an original backer of BRM, decided to go his own way. His early succession of cars went under the name of 'Thinwall Special', and were in reality thinly-disguised Ferraris. Various famous drivers, including Hawthorn, Collins, Taruffi and Farina, were to drive them.

The 'Thinwall' was frequently the principal BRM opponent in Formula Libre events. It is here seen in the hands of Farina, actually in the process of setting the first 100 mph lap record of Silverstone in 1953.

VII THE FORMULA TWO CHAMPIONSHIP YEARS 1952 & 1953

The prospects for motor racing at the start of 1952 did not seem encouraging. With the retirement of Alfa Romeo, Grand Prix organisers began switching to Formula Two (2-litres unsupercharged), in the hope of providing more varied competition for Ferrari. But some felt that F2 cars would seem tame in comparison with the previous years' contestants.

When Fangio had a serious accident whilst driving a Maserati at Monza – actually breaking his neck – this brought further gloom to racing prospects. However, there was to be at least one spark to lighten up the racing scene of 1952: a new star rising in the firmament to enliven motor racing in no mean manner. His name was John Michael Hawthorn.

Mike Hawthorn had been successful in club racing, driving both a Riley Sprite and an Imp. But his name was practically unknown to the general public. That was all to be changed at the 1952 Goodwood Easter Meeting. Hawthorn appeared behind the wheel of one of the new front-engined 2-litre Cooper Bristols, and the results were electrifying. No other driver could get near him, and overnight a new name was on the lips of the racing world.

Hawthorn was a real 'press on regardless' driver. He drove with tremendous style and verve, and often had the watchers on their toes from beginning to end of a race.

A year later, he was driving for Ferrari to become the first Englishman to secure a permanent place in a Continental Grand Prix team since Seaman joined Mercedes in 1937.

The young fresh-faced Mike Hawthorn in his new Cooper Bristol.

1952 International Trophy, Silverstone, Hawthorn demonstrates the 4-wheel drift in his Cooper Bristol, closely pursued by Jean Behra, Simca- *Gordini. Note the battered oil drum marker separating Hawthorn's car and the photographer's lens by about 8 feet!*

The dependable twin overhead cam engine developed 170 bhp.

1952

British Grand Prix Silverstone

Ferrari had not been caught napping by the change to Formula Two racing. Just as their twelve-cylinder Tipo 375 had proved victorious in 1951, so the new 2-litre Tipo 500 was to dominate the next two seasons of Grand Prix racing. In 1952 and 1953 the combination of this sturdy, reliable 4-cylinder racing car and the brilliant Alberto Ascari was to prove unbeatable, giving Ascari the World Championship in both years.

Piero Taruffi, third member of the successful all-Italian Ferrari team of 1952, in action. This picture illustrates the clean, uncluttered lines of the Tipo 500.

Ascari on the starting grid. He is wearing his famous blue racing helmet, which he always wore – apart from the day he was killed in 1955.

Coming out of Abbey Curve, the winner, Ascari, laps Dennis Poore in his Connaught. Poore finished a creditable fourth behind the Ferraris of Ascari and Taruffi, and Hawthorn's Cooper Bristol.

Note the 'protective' straw-bales for the massed crowds retained behind a single rope!

1953 International Trophy, Silverstone

Hawthorn, driving for Ferrari for the first time at Silverstone, collected most of the silverware. Moss, still without a worthy mount, had to be content with the Touring Car Trophy.

Hawthorn, always 'a bit of a lad', tries out a 'modified' windshield in the form of a Hepolite Piston 'for high performance' topless advert! Admiring spectators are Ken Wharton, Rivers Fletcher, and BARC Secretary John Morgan.

Man in Action

Often the greatest fun in watching our favourite sports comes from seeing the fine detail of how contestants perform – just how a tennis player serves, just how a soccer star kicks that winning goal.

With motor racing, it's a little more difficult to observe, particularly so today. Watching a modern Grand Prix driver at work, snugly enclosed in his personally-fitted tight cockpit, head covered by a flame-proof mask and huge safety helmet, only the eyes are really visible.

In the Fifties, you could see not only the driver's face, but actually watch his arms at work!

Duncan Hamilton indulges in a bit of 'wheel winding' with his HWM at Silverstone International Trophy Meeting in '53. Great stuff to watch, and photograph – more exciting, in fact, than some of the faster machinery.

Of course, the more difficult a car was to handle, or the more flamboyant a driver's style, the more 'action' one could see and enjoy.

1953 British Grand Prix

*Gonzalez' and Fangio's
Maseratis in the scrutineering
bay. On the left a Maserati
mechanic, hand on hip, seems to
be giving the scrutineer a
somewhat sceptical look!*

The start, with the Maseratis of Gonzalez and Fangio edging ahead of the Ascari and Hawthorn Ferraris. Ascari finally took the chequered flag more than a minute ahead of Fangio, illustrating Ferrari supremacy. The two leaders were, in fact, the only drivers to complete the full 90 laps of the Grand Prix; Farina and Gonzalez, trailing two laps astern.

Classic combination: Ascari drifts his Ferrari 500 through Woodcote. I always felt that if you put a coin in his tyre tracks he would touch it every time.

Stirling Moss and the Price of Patriotism

From his early racing days, Moss had nurtured the ambition to drive, and win, only in British cars. His patriotism was to cost him dear.

1952 Disappointment. The G-type ERA was manufactured by Moss' ex-Jaguar team-mate Leslie Johnson, who had bought the original ERA company. The G-type gave Moss a whole string of headaches. It was rather an ugly car, and another example of a sophisticated concept lacking sufficient backing to iron out the many bugs. This photograph was taken during the 1952 British Grand Prix, when it suffered from overheating and misfiring.

Right
1953 Problem Car No.1 The Cooper-Alta Special was built, in the main, by John Cooper (of 'The Autocar') and Ray Martin, who had combined to produce Moss' successful 500 cc Kieft. The (John) Cooper-Alta was powered by a 4-cylinder Alta engine, and was fitted with disc brakes – the first F2 car to use them. Once again, this was a problem vehicle. Initially, the engine wouldn't fit the chassis –

and the latter lacked rigidity. There were problems balancing the front disc brakes against the rear inboard drums, and the final drive leaked oil!

This car was quite a stylish looker, but looks don't win races! It is seen here at the reopening of the Crystal Palace Circuit in Coronation Year, 1953. Moss only managed fourth in his heat, and fifth in the final of the Coronation Trophy.

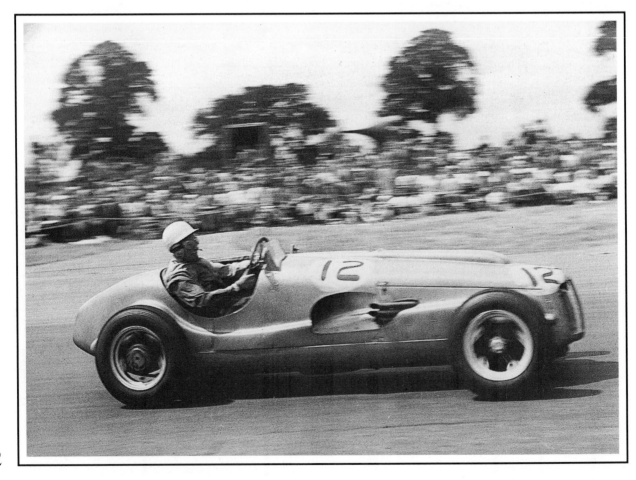

1953 Problem Car No. 2. The
Cooper-Alta Special, Mark
Two. This had a standard
Cooper F.2 chassis, with an engine fuelled by a nitro-
methane brew, which gave more power than the chassis
and small 15-inch Cooper wheels could cope with. The tyres
regularly disintegrated! However, some small successes were
forthcoming. Moss is seen here at the Crystal Palace, where he
won both heats in the London Trophy. It was great fun to watch
him in action, getting the best out of this
volatile little car.

Connaught at the Crystal Palace

Although lacking the ultimate performance of their better-financed Continental rivals in Formula Two racing, both HWM and Cooper had acquitted themselves well – on occasions to a surprising degree.

A third British manufacturer who had reason to be proud of his achievement on a modest budget was Connaught. These cars were built at Send in Surrey by Rodney Clarke, a highly-skilled engineer, with financial backing from Kenneth McAlpine, a member of the famous construction family, who was himself a keen racing driver.

The Connaught was more sophisticated than HWM or Cooper, but also heavier. It was powered by a Lea-Francis-based engine. The chassis was of tubular-ladder type construction, with front suspension by double wishbones, and torsion bars: At the rear end, there was a de Dion axle.

In 1953 Connaughts introduced fuel injection for the works cars. Works drivers that year included John Coombs, Ken McAlpine and Roy Salvadori.

Get in the queue – to shoot a Connaught! Photographers 'queue up' to get a shot at Ramp Bend, the sharp right-hander after the start.

Right
The author's own version from this viewpoint of Salvadori in his works Connaught – a study in concentration! During this race, the Crystal Trophy,

Salvadori set a new lap record. It is interesting to recall that Salvadori was at home in many different cars, sometimes driving four different types in four different races at one meeting.

He possessed the unusual ability to 'compartmentalise' his mind to the car he was driving at the moment, even when the brake and accelerator pedals were transposed, as in Maseratis. To my knowledge, he never put a foot wrong!

Tony Rolt, co-Le Mans winner for Jaguar in 1953, drove Rob Walker's immaculately-prepared navy blue Connaught in many events. The Walker/Rolt combination was most successful.

Here, Rolt is seen in action at 'The Palace', just one of the many venues where he brought home the bacon.

VIII NEW FORMULA CURTAIN-RAISERS

1954 was to be an auspicious year for motor racing on two counts. Firstly, the introduction of a new Formula One for Grand Prix cars, and secondly, at least equally exciting, the return of Daimler-Benz to Grand Prix racing after an absence of 14 years.

Mercedes intended to delay their debut until midsummer, but both Maserati and Ferrari were prepared to show their hand earlier in the season.

The new 250F Maserati was developed from the 6-cylinder 2-litre 1952/53 cars. It had a more powerful 2½-litre engine in a new tubular chassis, with de Dion rear axle. It also looked terrific – every inch a successful thoroughbred – and so it proved to be over several years.

Apart from the Works cars, the 250F was on sale to selected private customers. Among the first was Stirling Moss, who had at last given up his valiant yet unrewarding search for a worthy British-built Grand Prix mount.

Another private purchaser was Sid Greene of Gilby Engineering. This car was to be driven by Roy Salvadori, who had already been very successful with the Gilby 2-litre Maserati sports car.

Ferrari was fielding at least two Grand Prix permutations for the new Formula based on their successful 1952/53 Tipo 500. Firstly there was the conventional 2½-litre engined Tipo 625, which was virtually identical but for capacity to the 2-litre cars, plus a new design, the 553, later dubbed 'The Squalo' (whale). Squat and fitted with bulbous side fuel tanks, it was not exactly a thing of beauty. Its road-holding characteristics could be somewhat tricky, and only the ebullient Gonzalez seemed really at home in it.

1954 Goodwood Easter Monday meeting.
A sight to delight the eye of any enthusiast. Roy Salvadori, in the gleaming new green Maserati, gracing the starting grid against the Goodwood backdrop, which includes a classic ERA, and the sunlit Sussex Downs. Sid Greene sits perched on the rear wheel.

In 1954 Reg Parnell acquired the ex-Bobby Baird Ferrari, which had been rebuilt and fitted with a new 2½-litre engine.
This study in concentration shows Parnell hard at work during the Goodwood Whitsun Meeting. A most determined and experienced driver, he was always great fun to watch, not least when he was in contention with Salvadori's Maserati. These two could really provide some fireworks, and were, of course, old friends and Aston Martin sports car team mates.

*International Trophy
Silverstone, 1954.
Bulky Froilan Gonzalez, in
unusually contemplative mood,
as he sits hunched against the
elements in the new 553
'Squalo' Ferrari, waiting for the
start of his heat, which he won
without problem. Later, his
engine packed up, so he took
over Trintignant's conventional
625, to win the Final!*

69

Wet reflections of a typically unruffled Moss cornering his new 250F Maserati in the pouring rain. He finished third in his heat.

When purchasing the car, Moss requested at the outset that he wanted a right-hand throttle-pedal fitted instead of the traditional Maserati centre one. The Works' reaction was less than enthusiastic to this not unreasonable wish, but they did comply, grudgingly, in the end.

The 250F Maserati was a car held in the highest esteem by its drivers, including Moss. Behra, Fangio, Salvadori, Ascari, Villoresi, and Collins, shared his love of this car.

Its memory is cherished by drivers and public alike.

IX MERCEDES ARE BACK

Few occasions in the motor-racing of the Fifties caused such a buzz of excitement, such rumour, such speculation as the announcement that

Daimler-Benz were planning a return to Grand Prix motor racing in 1954.

The French Grand Prix 1954

Karl Kling takes one of the revolutionary 'Stromlinienwagen' past the pits during the opening practice session. We can see that, at this early stage, Mercedes had not even deigned

to sully the sweeping lines of the car with any number!

By the end of practice it was Fangio not unexpectedly, who had set fastest lap. This secured him not only pole position on

the starting grid but the added bonus, always given in this, the heart of the champagne country, of numerous crates of the local quality bubbly!

The questions being asked about Mercedes' return were legion: what would the cars look like? – visions of the 3-litre 1939 W154, also the beautiful 1½-litre W165 version which trounced the Alfas at Tripoli would spring to mind. Well, of course they wouldn't be like that – and anyway there was a spanking new Formula for 2½-litres unblown, or 750cc. blown. Might Mercedes even go for the latter? No one else had risked it, but the Germans were among the greatest experts with supercharged cars.

Who would the drivers be? Would Fangio be invited, or would it be an all-German team? Lastly, when and where would Mercedes make their dramatic return début – and it was sure to be dramatic. The motor-racing world was agog.

When it was at last announced that Daimler-Benz had chosen the French Grand Prix at Reims, scene of some of their most memorable pre-war victories, thousands of fans said: 'We must be there'. I said: 'Come hell or high water,

Boy, what a car! I heard this expression, or its equivalent, in a variety of languages, many times at Reims. Readers can reflect on this unobstructed view of mechanics at work on one of the new Mercedes in front of the pits.

I venture to suggest that, in similar circumstances today, the foreground would be black with spectators crowding round to get even the briefest glimpse of such an exciting racing car.

I'm not going to miss making *my* record of this piece of motor-racing history'.

I couldn't wait for the weeks to pass. Having arrived in Reims we were sipping drinks at a boulevard cafe in Place d'Erlon when Fangio, Karl Kling and Hans Hermann sat down at the next table. Of course, the team drivers had already been announced, but suddenly, this was it: the Mercedes team was here!

The Reims-Gueux circuit, just outside the town was a high-speed triangle, one of the two fastest genuine road-racing circuits in Europe – Spa-Francorchamps being the other.

Mercedes had designed their cars, or, at least, their aerodynamic bodywork, specifically with this circuit in mind. The unconventional appearance of the cars caused many a raised eyebrow as the practice sessions got under way, and when those gleaming silver bonnets were lifted, a lot more surprises were revealed!

In view of Mercedes' past reputation, it was not surprising that their design for the new W196 should be both very sophisticated and advanced – in fact, well ahead of its rivals.

Apart from the aerodynamic body, there were many innovative features. The chassis was of tubular space frame construction. Within it, the straight eight engine was turned through 70° to reduce height. It had desmodromic valve gear, and fuel injection. The 2496 cc engine developed 260 bhp at 8500 revs, and this power would eventually be stepped up to 290 bhp.

Suspension was independent all round, and included low-pivot swing axles at the rear.

Some people were surprised that Mercedes had not fitted disc brakes, but the company were not convinced by Jaguar's success with discs. Instead, Mercedes chose to fit massive inboard drum brakes so that they did not increase the unsprung weight. They can be seen very clearly in this picture.

16/4

What an atmosphere, with tension rising as the cars take their places on the starting grid, prior to the warming-up lap!

See who you can spot: In the foreground in front of the Gonzalez Ferrari, No. 2, we see Fangio chatting to Bira, with commentator James Tilling, prodding Bira in the rib!

To the right, in trilby hat, tie and white shirt, I think I see one-time world land speed record-holder Captain George Eyston. To the left of the gap, in the throng, Mike Hawthorn gives an admiring – or maybe apprehensive – glance at the German opposition.

Move to the left foreground, and we see, directing operations, or the most important part of them, the dominant figure of Alfred Neubauer, Mercedes' team manager. This day and its outcome probably meant more to him than to any other person present.

When is a Track Pass not a Track Pass?

Every motor racing photographer has his own favourite viewpoints round any given circuit. But there is one place where, quite naturally, all cameramen want to be at the start of a race, and that is on the Start Line.

So it was before the French Grand Prix at Reims in 1954. Excitement was running high: the cars were doing their warming up lap: officials, pit staff, journalists and photographers milling around, including myself.

All at once, I saw a line of gendarmes spreading out right across the circuit in front of the grid, and linking hands to form a solid line. They then proceeded to 'sweep' the circuit. Pressmen and photographers included were propelled onwards away from the grid – the vital scene of action. A track pass seemed to count for nought.

My heart was filled with dismay as this uniformed line marched inexorably towards me. There was no way past them.

Just then, a French film crew ahead of me made contact with the 'strong blue line'. 'Pathé' called the film men, and a gendarme waved them on. I was next in line. In desperation I, too, called out 'Pathé' and behold: Open Sesame: I was through!

The two wide-bodied silver Mercedes of Fangio and Kling give the impression of crowding out Ascari's 250F Maserati, as they accelerate off the start line.

Both Ascari and Villoresi had signed with Lancia to test and race the new D50 Grand Prix car which was in the pipeline. At this time, it was not yet ready, so the drivers were loaned to Maserati on a temporary basis. On this occasion, their efforts were not to be fruitful: Ascari retired, and Villoresi finished fifth.

As the two leading Mercedes sweep off the long high-speed back straight of the main Soissons-Reims road, Fangio leads into 60° Thillois hairpin, but team-mate Kling overdoes it, and takes to the escape road!

Gonzalez evacuates his smoking Ferrari after he burst an oil pipe whilst dicing with Hermann's Mercedes for third place. Hawthorn's Ferrari had already blown up attempting to stay with the Mercs.

Under a lowering sky the 'Silver Arrows' of Fangio and Kling dive flat out down the finishing straight from Thillois. At the end, Fangio led Kling across the line, to a 1 – 2 victory. Hans Hermann had retired, but not before he had set the fastest lap.

It was altogether an impressive return for Daimler-Benz.

Battle Resumes at Silverstone

On their showing at the French Grand Prix, it certainly looked as if Mercedes-Benz were all set to re-establish German supremacy in Grand Prix motor-racing as of yore.

Ferrari drivers Hawthorn and Gonzalez on conventional 625s made fast practice times, followed closely by Moss (250F Maserati). Near the end of practice, Fangio went out with a lightly-fuelled Mercedes, and, in spite of the car's problems, succeeded in making fastest time – in fact, the first 100 mph lap by a 2½-litre car – to share the front row of the grid with the two Ferraris and single Maserati. No one but the Master could have managed such a thing.

Three minutes to go, and a white-overalled capped Mercedes mechanic checks his watch. At the 'off' Gonzalez, Moss and Hawthorn beat Fangio away from the line.

Cause. This low-angled shot of the W196 central cockpit gives, more or less, the driver's view-point. Beyond the sharp outline of the aeroscreen, there rises the upward sweep of the all-enveloping bodywork, completely masking any sight of the car's front wheel. Small wonder that Fangio repeatedly clouted those marker tubs!

Quickest off the mark were the Ferraris of Hawthorn (11) and Gonzalez (9).

Effect. The streamlined Mercedes' bodywork, dented and battered from sundry encounters with marker drums on various Silverstone corners, as Fangio tries desperately to select a tight line in his hopeless pursuit of the flying Gonzalez.

For the next championship race two weeks later, the British Grand Prix at Silverstone, it was rumoured that Mercedes would produce their next rabbit out of the hat in the form of a more conventionally-bodied W196 suitable for slower, more twisty circuits.

But when the doors of the Daimler-Benz transporters were opened in Northants it was clear that the latest 'rabbit' was still under wraps in Stuttgart, and the streamlined cars were to be used again – this time on a very different sort of circuit from Reims.

It was soon evident that the all-enveloping bodied cars were going to prove quite a handful for their drivers – even for Fangio.

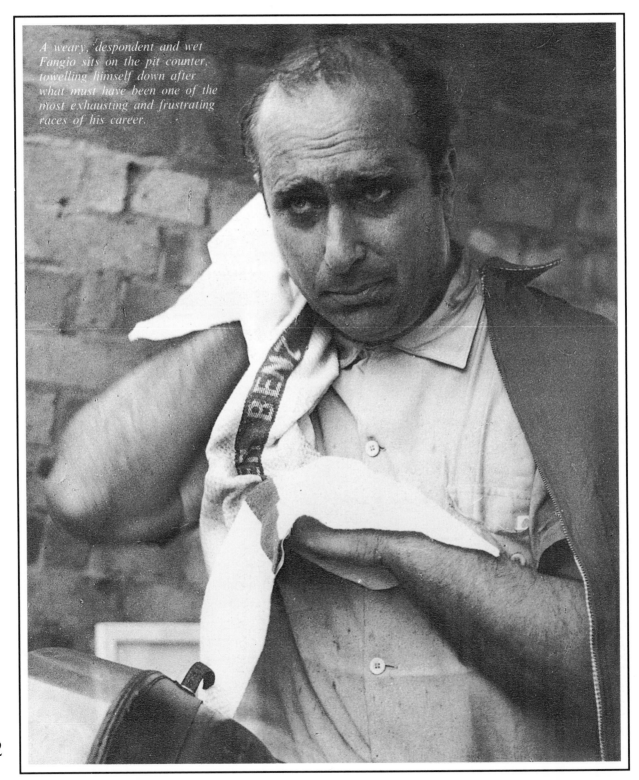

A weary, despondent and wet Fangio sits on the pit counter, towelling himself down after what must have been one of the most exhausting and frustrating races of his career.

The Team Manager

Many thumbnail sketches have been written of famous drivers, and even a few statues erected, but very little has been written, and fewer statues cast, of famous team managers.

If one were to try and select one such manager to represent the breed, it would surely have to be Alfred Neubauer of Mercedes – though it would need a very large block of granite from which to chisel his image!

Larger than life in all respects, Neubauer loomed over the Grand Prix scene for almost three decades. His management of Mercedes pre-war made him legendary, and his experience and expertise were second to none.

I saw him standing on a rain-soaked circuit at Berne in '51, when the Mercedes star had yet to re-emerge from the receding clouds of war, and their Italian arch rivals, Alfa, reigned supreme. Even then, one was conscious of the presence of this great man.

With Mercedes' return to motor-racing, Neubauer quickly re-occupied his long-vacant position as one of the dominant personalities of the sport.

Here we see him at the 1954 British GP in a typical stance – an impressive figure, stopwatch in hand, his attention riveted back down the road for the next glimpse of his cars to check their progress as they flashed by.

This was not to be one of Neubauer's days of glory, but whatever the race outcome he would do his job as only a true professional can.

Catch me if you can! Stowe Corner, with Gonzales' Ferrari, leader for the whole race and ultimate winner, in full cry. Team-mate Mike Hawthorn came second, after a tremendous scrap with Moss, which only ended when the Maserati broke a drive shaft when Moss was in second place.

A quite extraordinary feature of this race was that the F1 lap record was equalled by no less than 7 drivers, namely Gonzalez, Hawthorn, Moss, Fangio, Ascari (Maserati), Marimon (Maserati), and Behra (Gordini).

X DAWN CHORUS AT MONACO

One May evening in 1955, I drove into Monaco. It was my first visit, and I had come as a very excited young photographer to cover this most famous round-the-houses road race. One of my greatest ambitions was about to be fulfilled.

It was before the era of high-rise blocks, and I was struck by the almost Edwardian elegance of the Principality. Did they really allow racing through these narrow streets, I asked myself? I was soon to find out.

Practice was at an early hour next morning, and I was up and ready in good time, leaning out of my bedroom window, admiring the peaceful scene. I was quite unprepared for the shattering roar reverberating through the narrow streets as the first car to begin practice started up and moved off.

I rushed out and hurried towards the nearest vantage point on the circuit. Negotiating the narrow pavement beside The Mirabeau, I heard behind me the rising snarl of a racing engine bearing down on me at considerable velocity, and aiming, I reckoned, at the small of my back.

There came a quick 'WROOF' as the driver changed down. I glimpsed a flash of silver, and, barely an arm's length away, Fangio's W196 Mercedes accelerated past. Practice had begun in earnest. I was going to use a lot of film before breakfast!

Lancia had entered the lists with their new Grand Prix D50 at Barcelona the previous autumn, and had also competed in the first race of the 1955 season at Buenos Aires. The cars had proved very fast, but unreliable, and Lancia's only success so far had been at the Turin Grand Prix – a non-championship race.

Like Mercedes, Lancia had introduced several innovations to their design. It was the first V8 engine of the new formula – not that this was an innovation in itself – but for the first time the engine was to bear some of the stresses of the whole car. The most obvious innovation, of course, was the outrigger fuel tanks on either side of the body, which did not make for a sleek whole.

Now at Monaco, in the second round of the World Championship, Lancia were to try again to wrest some of the glory from Mercedes, who had been having things very much their own way.

Here we see, with early morning shadows streaking the roadway, Ascari swinging his Lancia into the Station Hairpin.

Louis Rosier (Maserati) leads Perdisa in a similar 250F, and Mike Hawthorn (Vanwall) through the snaking bends down from the Mirabeau.

Fangio putting on lock as he takes his Mercedes right into the kerbline on the acute Station Hairpin

Moss (Mercedes) follows Hawthorn's Vanwall through the Station Hairpin.

Lancia mechanics at work
before the start on the D50 V8
engine. Note the wire mesh on
the eight carburettor air intakes,
and how the mechanics have to
lean across the outrigger fuel
tanks.

A hand speaks louder than
words! Neubauer makes a point
during an earnest pre-race
discussion with Moss.

Rudi Caracciola, famed for his
many Mercedes victories of the
Thirties, leans on the pit
counter, reflecting perhaps, on
days of past glory. During
practice he had witnessed Fangio
shatter the eighteen-year-old
Monaco lap record which
'Caratsch' had set in 1938.

Starters at the ready, with Mercedes, Lancia, Mercedes, filling the front row of the grid.

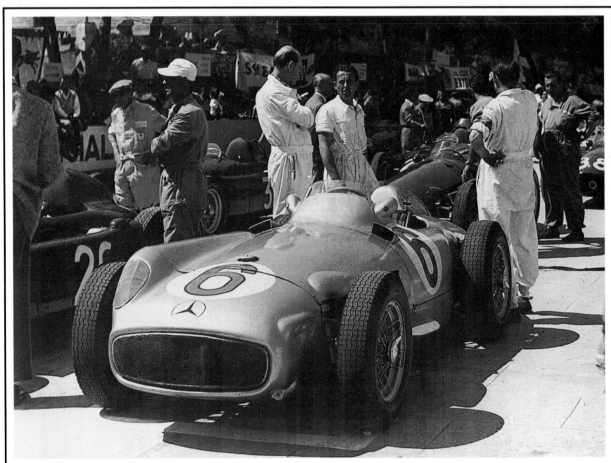

For sheer excitement, drama, and glamour Monaco has always been in a class of its own, particularly at the start.

In the Fifties, this took place on the

Moss' Mercedes, backed by white-overalled mechanics, stands waiting on the grid. For this race, both Fangio and Moss were driving new short wheelbase cars, fitted with outboard front brakes.

promenade, where, at other times, people would stroll at leisure, drinking-in this beautiful setting. A narrow strip of shrubbery separates the promenade from the back straight behind, and this accommodates the pits. Today, of course, the start line is on this back straight.

In this scene, the atmosphere is electrifying, as engine notes rise to a crescendo before the flag falls. The sundrenched spectators, massed in the temporary stands backing the harbour, crane forward to get a better view. Ascari (Lancia), sandwiched between the Mercedes of Fangio and Moss, leads off the line by a coat of paint!

91

Every photographer has his dreams – here was one of mine fulfilled!

A summer's afternoon in Monaco: a delightful cooling breeze ruffles the waters of the harbour, and my idol, Fangio, in the lead with his silver W196 Mercedes, is in my lens, with superb lighting conditions, as he rounds the Virage des Gazomètres. This was, for me, a mini-second of sheer magic!

93

Mercedes pit signals on the back straight as Fangio's car shoots into view (extreme left picture). A few laps later, he was out. Neubauer supervises anxiously from atop the pit counter.

94

Compare this 'cross-arms' shot of Trintignant (Ferrrari), the ultimate winner, rounding the Virage des Gazomètres, with the picture of Fangio just a few feet further round the same 180° turn. In the latter shot, there was no obvious sight of arm movement: was Fangio already on full lock and letting the wheel run back through his hands, or was he changing gear? No answers on postcards, please!

Although a curse to the drivers, part of the excitement of Monaco for spectators is the drama of light and shade, as cars flash from deep shadow into brilliant sunshine. Here, Taruffi (Supersqualo Ferrari), erupts from the shaded roadway into a patch of sunlight before Ste. Dévote.

For one Mercedes to blow up was exceptional. When Moss' car went the same way in a

cloud of smoke a few laps later, the unthinkable had happened to Daimler-Benz!

Lengthening shadows, as Trintignant sweeps through Ste. Dévote en route to a totally unexpected victory for both him and Ferrari.

Alberto Ascari

Trying all he knew to catch the Mercedes of Fangio and Moss, Ascari made a most dramatic and uncharacteristic mistake. Shooting out of the tunnel on to the quay, he overdid it: his Lancia cannoned into some straw bales, and then a stone bollard. The car ricocheted off straight into the harbour. To the consternation of spectators, both car and driver disappeared in a cloud of steam, to be followed by sighs of relief as the familiar Ascari blue helmet bobbed to the surface, and he was hauled aboard a rescue boat.

It appeared that Ascari had suffered nothing worse than an unexpected ducking, plus shock.

Strolling by the harbour that evening, I took this picture. The big Lancia transporter waits at the quayside to collect Ascari's wrecked car as it is winched from the water.

The next day, we crossed into Italy for a holiday at Alassio. A few days later, passing a news stand, my eye happened to catch the headline blazed across an Italian newspaper 'ASCARI MORTO'. It could not be true – hadn't I seen him myself a few days previously? But of course, it was true.

He had been killed at Monza testing a Ferrari sports car – really just by chance. Whether or not the after-effects of Ascari's Monaco accident had any bearing on his untimely end was, and will remain, one of the mysteries of motor-racing.

So passed one of the greatest racing drivers of that, or any other, era. We who saw him drive were privileged.

XI THE BRITISH ENGAGE TOP GEAR

In addition to Ascari's death, another terrible happening had cast a black cloud over motor-racing in 1955. Namely, the grim disaster at Le Mans in which two drivers and many spectators were killed or injured.

This called into question the whole subject of motor-racing safety, and was instrumental in leading, ultimately, to much-needed improvements in safety for spectators and drivers alike.

At the end of the 1955 season, Daimler-Benz announced their retirement from racing – maybe the Le Mans disaster had some influence on their decision, but Mercedes had won pretty well all that was worth winning in the past two years, so, logically, this was a good time to pull out.

Ascari was gone, and Lancia weighed down by the swingeing costs of their Grand Prix development, had transferred their racing cars, lock, stock and barrel, to Ferrari.

1956 dawned, not only as a new year, but with a new racing scene.

In the completely changed situation, there was a general post of drivers: Fangio joined Ferrari, together with Peter Collins and ex-Lancia driver Castelotti. Moss became No.1 for the Maserati Works team, and Hawthorn joined BRM, who were starting to get their act together with a fast, if somewhat temperamental, car.

Goodwood Easter Monday 1956 was one of the first race meetings of the new season. It was always quite an occasion – an apéritif for things to come!

Connaught had brought along two new Works 'Syracuse' cars for Bob Gerard and Archie Scott-Brown. 'Syracuse' came from Connaught's most successful excursion into Formula One the previous autumn. Tony Brooks had won the Syracuse Grand Prix for Connaught against the Works Maserati team. This was the first British car/driver Grand Prix win since Sir Henry Seagrave won at San Sebastian in 1924!

Here we see the start of the Glover Trophy race: Bob Gerard (Connaught), nearest camera: Hawthorn (P25 BRM), a tissue ahead: Scott-Brown (Connaught): Moss (Maserati).

Moss, in a new works fuel-injection 250F Maserati, won, after a terrific scrap with Archie Scott-Brown. The latter was a remarkable driver, who, in spite of a physical disability with one of his hands, was both incredibly fast and consistent.

Straws in the Wind

In 1953, Tony Vandervell developed his own British car, the Vanwall Special, later shortened to Vanwall. It was initially fitted with a 2-litre engine, but by 1955 improvements included a 2½-litre unit. Once again, Vandervell employed a selection of talented drivers, including Hawthorn, Tony Brooks, Ken Wharton, and later in 1955 Harry Schell, who had come over from Ferrari.

Schell was one of the most amusing and charismatic personalities ever to sit behind the wheel of a racing car, and he was a very competent driver to boot.

The 1955 Vanwalls were undoubtedly fast, but often failed to finish, due to a succession of mechanical problems. Furthermore, both Wharton and Brooks had hair-raising escapes when their cars caught fire. Nevertheless it was clear that Vanwalls could, one day, and maybe soon, become a force to be reckoned with in Grand Prix racing.

*Waiting for the 'off', Behra and   By the end of the first lap,
Moss have yet to fit their   Moss led from Behra, Brooks,
goggles. Brooks is at the ready.   Hawthorn and Collins.*

The clean lines of the 1955
Vanwall show well against the
dark background of trees, as
Schell hustles the car through
The Glade at the Crystal
Palace.

Having cornered the 500 cc. market and been very successful with their front-engined F2 Cooper-Bristol, the little Cooper car company decided in 1956 to introduce a new rear-engined F2 car. It was powered by a Coventry Climax engine, developed from the original Climax fire pump power unit.

Salvadori tested the car at Goodwood immediately before the British Grand Prix race day at Silverstone.

Roy Salvadori and John Cooper borrow a coil from a friendly 1929 Austin Seven, when they required a replacement part for the Cooper!

Next day, Salvadori had a convincing win with this car in the Formula Two Silverstone race.

The successes by Vanwall and Cooper at Silverstone, not forgetting BRM too – Hawthorn led at the start of the International Trophy – were pretty hefty straws in the wind. British drivers, and now British cars, if they could master reliability, were elbowing their way to the fore in Formula One and Formula Two to match our already-established sports car successes.

Vanwall 1956

Since the previous year, the Vanwall had been completely redesigned by Lotus chief Colin Chapman, in co-operation with aerodynamics specialist Frank Costin. The fuel-injection 4-cylinder engine produced around 290 bhp, disc brakes were fitted, and the car had new 'teardrop' low drag bodywork, the latter compensating for the fact that the car was unusually high, due to the transmission design.

Schell had elected to stay with Vanwall for the 1956 season. When Maserati declined to enter for the early May International Trophy, it was agreed that Moss could also drive for Vanwall at Silverstone.

Practice produced some startling results. Moss and Schell were fastest in spite of great efforts by Fangio in his Lancia-Ferrari. Mike Hawthorn was also very quick in his BRM P25.

Seen here is the first rank lineup: Vanwall, Vanwall, Lancia-Ferrari, BRM – three British cars out of the first four.

With only 30 seconds to go, and the tension rising, look at the grins on the driver's faces. What was the momentary non-vocal joke they were sharing? Some sign by that wag Harry Schell? It's a pity that we can't see Moss' face, because by the end of the race he was certainly beaming!

Moss victorious, and with a British car. So one of his greatest ambitions was fulfilled. Among the smiling well-wishers note Colin Chapman, in cap and check shirt. His work had not been in vain.

Although this was not a full-length Grand Prix, Moss in the Vanwall had beaten the foreign best.

Another newcomer to the Ferrari team that year was Peter Collins, seen here in his starting position on the second row. When Fangio's car broke in pursuit of Moss, Collins was flagged in and Fangio took over, but that car also melted under the strain!

XII THE OLD MASTER AT WORK

The British Grand Prix 1956

British enthusiasts were agog to see if Vanwall could produce a repeat performance of their victory over Ferrari at Silverstone in May.

Of course, with Moss now committed to Maserati, accompanied by Jean Behra, Vanwall had brought in Gonzalez and Trintignant to partner Schell. Hawthorn had Tony Brooks and Ron Flockhart supporting him in the BRM team, whilst Ferrari were fielding a full complement consisting of Fangio, Collins, Castellotti, and the Marquis de Portago.

BRM Équipe. Spectators gaze at the Works BRM P25s cordoned off by a single rope in a corner of the paddock, and watched over by BRM father figure, Raymond Mays.

*Unblemished, things of beauty –
lined up in the paddock before
the race, unscarred by the
graffiti advertising of later years
– four classic racing cars, a
Vanwall and three Ferraris.*

The P25 BRM engine – potent when reliable!

A happy and hopeful Moss helps Bertocchi push his 250F down to the starting grid.

Peter Collins, a veteran of Silverstone and leading the World Championship at this stage, gives some advice to Ferrari team-mate Castellotti, a newcomer to the circuit.

Fingertip steering, as Fangio guides his Ferrari towards the start line. His goggles and helmet rest on the side fuel tank fairing.

109

The start. A near-repetition of the May Silverstone, as, from a front rank of Moss, Fangio, Hawthorn and Collins, Hawthorn's BRM blasts into the lead. The Ferraris of Fangio and Collins are about level, with Moss' Maserati (7) and Gonzalez' Vanwall (18) next. Brooks, BRM number 24, is just behind. By the end of the first lap, Brooks was sitting on Hawthorn's tail – BRMs lying 1 and 2!

His tall figure high in the slim BRM, Hawthorn in full flight during the early stages. Here he takes it close to the wooden board and oil drum corner-liner – Armco barriers were still a thing of the future.

Unfortunately, once again British cars were back to their old unreliability, when their drivers had battled to the front. BRMs went out, so did Vanwalls. Only Connaught's fourth place (Jack Fairman) brought slight British consolation.

When Ferrari No.2 (Collins) failed, No.4 driver (de Portago) was flagged in for Collins to take over.

Here we see the next Ferrari 'all change': Picture One. A disgruntled Castelotti brings his ailing car in for a pit stop, and under goes the jack: to the right of his head, we see the disconsolate face of car-less de Portago.

111

Picture Two. 'Let me have a go!' No second bidding required for de Portago, as he leaps into the battered, but vacant, Ferrari. A few laps later, that car broke. But de Portago did have the consolation of sharing second place with Collins, who, remember, had taken over the Spaniard's car No.4. Complicated, isn't it?

After the BRM failure, the Works Maserati of Moss, followed by Salvadori's Gilby Maser led 1-2 for a time, but Fangio was putting on the pressure. Here he is back in his familiar position, in the lead!

Juan Manuel Fangio

How does one write about this extraordinary racing driver? It has all been said before, and many times over. A legend in his lifetime? Yes, in fact, a legend over these past thirty-odd years since his retirement. The image does not dim or tarnish. The greatest racing driver ever? Who can say? BUT I always notice that even the most hard-bitten motor journalists of the present decade who have seen him at the wheel of a racing car at some 'demonstration' event are still awed by his magic.

For me, it was, and always will be, one *helluva* kick that I had the chance to watch Fangio and photograph him in action: lucky devil!

Look – no hands! A 'both hands off ' salute from the usually undemonstrative Fangio is returned by his mechanic as the victor flashes past his pit, having taken the chequered flag once again.

A joyous reception for 'the Maestro' from his wife and pit staff as he coasts to a halt.

This was Fangio's last win in Britain: he would come here to race only once more – at

Aintree in 1957, his final Grand Prix year.

XIII AINTREE GRAND NATIONAL

The Aintree Circuit was to me, something of an anachronism. Sited within the environs of the famous Grand National steeplechase course, it seemed to retain something of the atmosphere from that entirely different sport, even when motor racing was the order of the day.

Besides this, many of the public facilities, however good, spoke of an entirely different age. These facilities included the main grandstand, which overlooked not only the start and finish line of the motor-racing circuit but the 'hallowed' turf behind.

Against the background of the colonnaded period Aintree grandstand, with ten minutes to go, mechanics, pressmen, officials and photographers mill round the waiting cars. In the foreground are the Ferraris of Collins (12) and Hawthorn (10). Most of the drivers seem to be momentarily occupied elsewhere!

Watching from the main stand as Grand Prix cars were wheeled out on to the starting grid below, one sometimes felt a slight suspicion that on the grass a few feet away a string of eques-

View across the Aintree starting grid for the 1957 Grand Prix d'Europe, with the 'hallowed' turf in the immediate background. No.16 is Trintignant's Ferrari: the driver has just wandered over towards Harry Schell's Maserati, No.6. Schell stands three-quarter back to the camera. To the right of the picture is Ferrari driver Musso.

trian contenders might also suddenly appear to challenge the prancing horse of Ferrari – and the rest!

Its slightly unusual atmosphere aside, Aintree was to provide some exciting and memorable motor racing. In 1955, Stirling Moss had led team-mate Fangio's Mercedes across the finishing line to a well-deserved victory. Let there be no mistake about it: no driver could win from Fangio unless he was worthy and capable of the victory.

In 1957, Fangio had returned to the Maserati fold after a successful but somewhat abrasive previous year with Ferrari. Supporting him as Maserati's No.2 was the volatile but talented Frenchman, Jean Behra.

Hawthorn was back with Ferrari, alongside Peter Collins, the start of their great two-season 'Mon Ami Mate' friendship and partnership.

For the new season Vanwall had Moss, Tony Brooks, and newcomer Stuart Lewis-Evans, who, having proved himself at Reims, was driving No.3. Unfortunately neither Moss nor Brooks was 100% fit – Moss was suffering from a sinus infection, and Brooks was still recovering from a crash whilst driving for Aston Martin at Le Mans.

117

Breeding will out. Three thoroughbreds line up at the front: Vanwall, Maserati, Vanwall; mounts of Brooks, Behra, Moss.

This was one of only three Grand Prix occasions when Fangio was not a front-liner. He was in the second row.

Rounding Tatts, Brooks has the Ferraris of Hawthorn and Collins breathing down his neck.

Moss led Behra for twenty laps. Then Moss' engine started to miss. The Vanwall pit called in Brooks, and Moss jumped into the latter's car, and went off like a scalded cat. This emergency move had been arranged in advance, as Tony Brooks was so under par. But now Moss was back in 9th place, and Jean Behra, seen here, with flapping fuel filler cap, was in the lead.

Study in determination:
Hawthorn in pursuit of Behra.

No less determined was Collins,
chasing team-mate Hawthorn,
seen here as he takes the
Melling Crossing.

Moss, most determined of all,
quickly moved from 9th up to
7th, and then started to 'gobble
up' all and sundry in his bid to
recapture the lead.

Gallant Tony Brooks was having a go with Moss' 'wonky' car.

For Fangio this was just not his day.

When the throttle linkage broke on his Vanwall, Stuart Lewis-Evans stopped to fix it out on the circuit. He then re-started, and finished the race, minus bonnet.

Now in the lead, with the chequered flag in sight, Moss glances back as he accelerates out of Tatts en route to a famous victory.

Moss and Brooks became the first British drivers jointly to win a Grande Épreuve for over thirty years.

And that was not all for the British. Roy Salvadori, in the little Works Cooper (right), fitted with a two-litre Climax engine, had been involved in a great scrap with Trintignant's Ferrari. Roy eventually passed the Frenchman into 4th place, only to have the Cooper's gearbox blow up a few laps later. Nothing daunted, Salvadori pushed his car to the finishing line to take fifth place, and become the first driver ever to score Drivers' Championship points in a rear-engined car.

What a day's sport for this country to remember!

XIV SIGN FROM SURBITON

One Sunday in early May of 1957, I received a telephone call from a motor-racing journalist, Gerry Ames. Could I get over quickly to the Cooper Car Company works at Surbiton? They were preparing a 2.2 Climax-engined car for Australian Jack Brabham to race in the Monaco Grand Prix the following Sunday. Ames wanted some pictures quickly to send to Australia.

I grabbed my camera and flash gun and drove over. I had never been in the tiny Cooper works before, and had only seen Brabham briefly, and at a distance. It was several minutes before I realised that the mechanic in stained brown overalls, working assiduously beside the pipe-smoking John Cooper, was the potential Grand Prix driver himself!

There were sceptics who said that the car would never even qualify, but qualify it certainly did, and, 100 laps into the race, with only 5 to go, Brabham was lying third. With Cooper prospects so high, the fuel pump went, but Brabham pushed his car over the line to finish sixth.

The performance of the modest Cooper in Brabham's hands was a real eye-opener, and a fresh warning to the established Grand Prix teams of things to come.

XV A MEMORABLE YEAR – 1958

Easter Monday, Goodwood

1958 was to be a most memorable year for British drivers, although regrettably tinged with sadness.

Britons now dominated every branch of the sport, right up to the very top. Indeed, Grand Prix racing would have been in a very sorry state

The Glover Trophy was the principal event of the day for Formula One cars. Moss is in pole position, then Behra (BRM), with Hawthorn's Ferrari on the outside.

Unluckily for Moss, he stalled his engine a split second before the start. He then had his engine blow up whilst in hot pursuit of the leaders, Behra, Hawthorn, and Brabham. Behra

crashed his BRM, and Hawthorn (Ferrari) was the winner, the Coopers of Brabham and Salvadori finishing second and third respectively.

Hawthorn on the way to winning the Glover Trophy. It can be noted that the completely new 246 Dino had, quite apart from mechanical factors, little external resemblance to the 1957 Ferraris.

One minute to go, and the cars are lined up for the Formula Two race. Jack Brabham's rear-engined Cooper is No.20, and behind Cliff Allison's front-engined Lotus is No.22. Colin Chapman had yet to decide to 'switch ends'!

without the British, for they were the backbone of the racing teams.

Leading Ferrari were Hawthorn and Collins: Moss led Vanwall, backed up by Brooks and Stuart Lewis-Evans: Cooper could rely on Salvadori and Australia's Brabham, Connaught had Archie Scott-Brown and Jack Fairman, while Lotus, yet to reach full flower, had among its drivers future champion Graham Hill.

At the beginning of 1958, new regulations came into force banning alcohol fuel, and substituting AvGas aviation spirit.

Both Vanwall and BRM had to adapt their engines to the fuel change, and were not ready for the Argentine Grand Prix in January.

Ferrari, on the other hand, had a completely new car, the V6 Dino 246, designed to use AvGas.

It had been agreed that Moss could drive for Rob Walker in events where Vanwall were not participating. Walker decided to send his Cooper to the Argentine for Moss. The engine had been enlarged to 2.2 litres by Alf Francis, who also quickly converted it to run on the new fuel.

It had looked as if Ferrari, who were fielding a full team, would have a walkover, but to everyone's amazement, Moss won, beating Luigi Musso's Ferrari into second place, with Hawthorn third.

For the British season opener on Easter Monday at Goodwood, Moss was again driving Rob Walker's Cooper, and Hawthorn came with a 246 Dino, so enthusiasts had high hopes that they might see 'giant-killer' Moss repeat his victory over Ferrari.

Harry Ferguson, of Ferguson Tractors, chats to Stirling Moss across the Rob Walker Cooper. Could they have been discussing 4-wheel drive? In the future (1961), when Tony Rolt was head of Ferguson research, they were to produce a 1½-litre 4-wheel drive racing car, which Moss was to drive with some success.

Daily Express International Trophy Silverstone

Down on the starting grid, a mechanic carries out a last-minute check on the tyres of Collins' Ferrari.

Master Mechanic

However fast a racing car may be potentially, and however good the man behind the wheel, there is little hope of being first at the chequered flag unless the back-up pit staff, including mechanics, is also of the highest order.

One man who was most certainly in the very top flight in this sphere was Moss' mechanic for many years, Alf Francis.

Francis came to Moss from HWM, and over the years travelled the world with him to many different racing circuits, oft-times burning the midnight oil the whole night through to ensure that his driver's car reached the starting line with the best possible chance of success.

The range of cars which Alf Francis worked on, repaired, rebuilt or built up from scratch for Moss was truly formidable. These included HWMs, various Coopers, 250F Maseratis, BRM and Lotus – this list does not, of course, include the many sports cars.

Moss had such faith in Alf Francis that he would send him out to supervise modifications on his car, as in the case of his first 250F Maserati.

When Moss started to drive for Rob Walker, it was Francis who took charge of the cars, and once again played his not inconsiderable part in Moss' successes.

Seen together here with the Rob Walker Cooper Climax on the starting grid of the 1958 International Trophy at Silverstone.

Silverstone International Trophy

Vanwall were once again absent, sorting out problems with their Bosch fuel-injection conversion to AvGas.

On the other hand, the lone Dino Ferrari entry, in the hands of Peter Collins, was again having problems from the cheeky Cooper brigade of Salvadori and Brabham, plus Moss on the Walker car, who had made best practice times in that order. Collins' Ferrari, although on the front rank, could only claim the outside of the grid!

However, at the drop of the flag, Salvadori and Moss made bad starts, Brabham led, but Collins soon went out in front, followed by Behra's BRM.

Collins, with his head well outside the protective screen, has his eyes glued to his inner front wheel and the apex of the corner, as he takes Copse. Collins won, but Salvadori took second place, to show yet again how the Coopers, in the right hands, and costing a fraction the price of most Grand Prix cars, could worry the pants off the likes of Ferrari!

British Grand Prix, Silverstone

By mid-July, when the Grand Prix 'circus' moved back to Silverstone, the Vanwall-Ferrari battle was in full swing – Vanwall having scored two Firsts and one Second – Ferrari one First and two Seconds, in addition to other placings for both teams.

Fangio had retired, and Maserati were no longer a force to be reckoned with. On the other hand, BRMs had pulled their socks up and taken second and third places in the Dutch Grand Prix. Coopers, still with a smaller engine, were nevertheless posing an ever-increasing threat to the supremacy of the larger front-engined cars.

Moss and Hawthorn before the start of the race. The main interest was focusing on these two great British drivers, and the unfolding drama of their struggle for the Drivers' World Championship.

An unbelievable sight only a few years ago: three British cars to one Italian line up on the front row of the grid. Hawthorn's Ferrari takes the outside position to the Cooper of Salvadori, the BRM of Schell, and the Vanwall of Moss (in pole position).

BUT chickens should never be counted too early. It was Collins' Ferrari, from the second row, which rocketed through into the lead in the first lap!

Moss tries his damnedest to catch the runaway Ferrari of Collins, but to no avail. In the end, the Vanwall's engine blew up under the strain!

133

Collins, No.1, drifting through Woodcote. He held his lead right from the first lap through to the chequered flag.

It can be seen from this picture that Collins was happy with the full wrap-round windshield, plus a small aero-screen. In contrast, his pal Hawthorn always opted for aero-screen only.

Hawthorn, No.2, captured by the camera, taking Woodcote at approximately the same point as the Collins shot, came in second – a great day for 'Mon-Ami-Mates'. It was Collins' last victory: in fact, his last complete race. Two weeks later, during the German Grand Prix at Nürburgring he crashed fatally.

Peter Collins

Collins, seen here before the start of the 1958 British Grand Prix, had, like Moss, been weaned on 500cc racing. He progressed to become a valued member of the Aston Martin sports car team. Tony Vandervell gave him a chance to drive the Thinwall Special, and later to become the first driver of the embryo Vanwall.

In 1955, he joined the Owen organisation, and was successful with their 250F Maserati, fitted with disc brakes, winning the International Trophy.

His biggest chances came when, in 1956, he joined the Ferrari team as second string to Fangio. Like Moss with Mercedes, Collins found that he learnt much by following the 'Maestro'. At the Italian Grand Prix, when Fangio's car failed, Collins performed a great act of selfless sportsmanship by handing over his car, and perhaps his chance of the World Championship.

Collins was one of the few drivers to be befriended by Enzo Ferrari, who had a very high opinion of the young driver, and Enzo was sparing indeed with his high opinions!

Collins' death was a loss, not only to his friend Hawthorn and the Ferrari team, but to Britain and the whole racing world.

Putting The Brakes On

In 1958, Enzo Ferrari still had an aversion to disc brakes, which was not shared by his British drivers, Collins and Hawthorn.

Whilst in England in the spring, Peter Collins had persuaded Dunlop to fit their discs to his beautiful new black Ferrari drop-head coupé, which was fresh from the Geneva Motor Show. Being on good terms with Enzo Ferrari, Collins hoped to convince the Commendatore of the disc's efficacy.

After Collins' death, and before the Italian Grand Prix, Mike Hawthorn, conscious of the braking advantage which discs gave to the Vanwalls, and anxious to be upsides, particularly with Moss, had the discs transferred from the ex-Collins' coupé to his Grand Prix Dino.

This was not the end of the matter. When the Vanwall camp heard that their principal rival now had a car, fitted with the same discs, they were anything but pleased. But, apart from a great deal of wrangling, in the end there was little they could do about it. The discs for Ferrari, as supplied to Collins, had been bought and paid for, and that was the end of the matter.

135

Moss, in earnest conversation with one of the Vanwall mechanics just before the race.

As the cars start to take their places under a blistering sun, American Phil Hill, newcomer to the Ferrari team, walks across behind his car (in the second row). Hill was to prove a very worthwhile addition to the Ferrari team right from the start.

1958 Italian Grand Prix, Monza

Ten seconds to the drop of the flag: a Ferrari mechanic, with arms aloft, gives the countdown on his fingers.

The 'eyes right' of the Ferrari mechanic is to pick up the team manager's signals, which the minion then transmits. Ferrari drivers watch him – and 'blow the starting flag'!

Hawthorn is sandwiched between the three Vanwalls of Moss, Brooks and Lewis-Evans.

Moss did one of his seemingly jet-propelled starts, to snatch the initial lead.

Over the years, Monza, perhaps more than any other circuit, has presented Grand Prix motor racing in the impressive manner, with speed, drama, excitement and maybe a touch of Italian Grand Opera thrown in!

Of course, because the Italian Grand Prix usually comes near the end of the season, when the Drivers' World Championship is reaching its peak, this certainly adds more than a touch of spicy Milanese sauce to the occasion!

The main grandstand, overlooking the start area and pits, is an impressive affair.

Tail-end view, with the three Vanwalls leading. But Phil Hill, Ferrari, No.18, extreme right, is in the process of rocketing through from the second row past team-mate Hawthorn, (No,14), to take the lead by the end of the first lap.

Hawthorn has passed Lewis-Evans, and is in pursuit of Moss, who now leads.

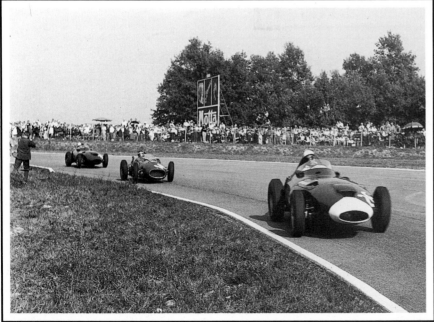

Lap Ten, at the South Curve. Vanwall-Ferrari-Vanwall: Moss leads Hawthorn, who leads Lewis-Evans.

On lap 61, Brooks, Vanwall, who had played a waiting and watching game, passed Hawthorn's Ferrari into the lead. Eleven laps later, the green car took the chequered flag to win this most exciting Italian Grand Prix.

This was Brooks' third win for Vanwall that year, having already won both the Belgian and the German Grand prix. He was to end the year a well-deserved third in the World Drivers' Championship.

Definitely at his best in a front-engined car, this modest young dental student, with his natural driving style, was rated by Moss as 'the greatest little-known driver of all time'.

Championship Profiles

The two principal contenders for the 1958 Drivers' World Championship were both British, and both outstanding drivers, but there the resemblance ended.

Mike Hawthorn had the quality of a shooting star – sometimes brilliant and travelling at very high speed. He'd been nicknamed 'The Farnham Flyer'.

Here, the 'press-on' determination shows on his face as Hawthorn corners the 246 Dino during the British Grand Prix at Silverstone in 1958 – his Championship Year.

His arrival on the motor-racing scene that Easter Monday at Goodwood in 1952 was both dramatic and totally unexpected.

His retirement from racing six years later, only weeks after becoming World Champion, and his fatal road accident so soon after that, was not only sad but also very dramatic.

In those few racing years, Hawthorn became one of the select 'top-notchers' of motor sport. His fortunes were, in the main, linked to Ferrari, and among his great victories he is particularly remembered for his fantastic scrap with and win over Fangio in the 1953 French Grand Prix.

The loss of his great friend, Peter Collins, came as a particularly bitter blow to Mike Hawthorn when he was battling to hold his points lead in the World Championship.

Setting aside the undoubted faults in the scoring system that year, Hawthorn still had to be some driver to even get within striking distance of the title.

Stirling Moss

Profile of a classic combination in action: Moss and Vanwall. The illogical scoring in the points system for the 1958 World Drivers' Championship were largely responsible for the title eluding him yet again. For the fourth consecutive year, Moss was runner-up.

Hopefully, there was some consolation for this driver who set such great store by winning in a British car. With his four wins and one second place for Vanwall, he led his team-mates, Brooks and Lewis-Evans, to take the World Formula One Constructors' Championship for the British company.

Looking back on Moss' memorable career, it is all too easy to recall just his victories.

Although they make a truly formidable list, and Moss was always the paramount example of a driver who went all out to win every race he entered, this is but part of the whole.

Moss was equally formidable, and successful, in any class of car: '500s', sports cars, Formula Two, or Grand Prix cars – front or rear-engined.

Moss was the ultimate never-say-die contestant. He was frequently at his most dangerous when all the odds were stacked against him: in fact, some of his greatest victories were won in such circumstances.

Lastly, I would wager that, in the course of his brilliant and action-packed career, Moss was probably responsible for more moments of really nail-biting excitement worthy of recall by the pen, in the mind, or on film, than any racing driver before or since.

XVI CHANGE AT LAST . . .

Friends and Rivals

Salvadori and Brabham: Cooper versus Aston-Martin

For the 1959 season, Cooper had been promised a full 2½-litre twin cam engine from Coventry Climax, and they naturally wanted Brabham and Salvadori, their most experienced and successful drivers, as their team for 1959.

However, Aston-Martin had decided to enter the Grand Prix arena that season with the new single-seater DBR4, and had already asked both Brabham and Salvadori to drive for them.

Brabham favoured Cooper, and had no other allegiance, but Salvadori was torn over his decision, as he had driven for the Aston-Martin works sports car team since '53, and so felt a strong bond with Astons.

In the end, the two friends decided that they must go their separate ways – Brabham to Cooper (rear-engined), Salvadori to front-engined Aston-Martin. These decisions proved crucial for both drivers.

End of a Decade

Considerable changes in the Grand Prix scene as the old season gave way to the new had now come to be accepted as the norm.

In May 1959, the Daily Express International Trophy was expected, as in previous years, to give an insight into the relative merits and prospects of both the Grand Prix drivers and cars facing a fresh season.

Yet few people could have foreseen the true significance of the front-rank line-up for that race, and its outcome.

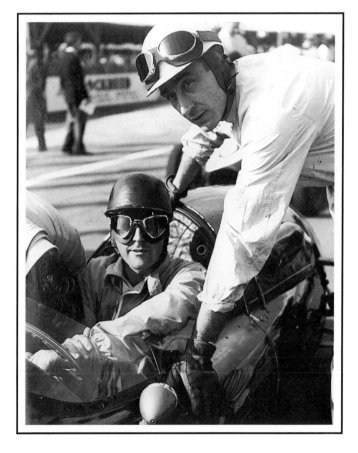

Four premier racing drivers: Moss, Brooks, Salvadori, and Brabham, headed the grid. Three of them were in the latest front-engined Grand Prix cars (Moss in a BRM, now, at last, really competitive: Brooks in the latest Dino Ferrari, from the most famous racing car manufacturer in Europe, and Salvadori in the newest Grand Prix contender, the DBR4 single-seater Aston Martin in its first race.)

141

Their passing

In addition, on the outside of the grid, was Jack Brabham in the works rear-engined Cooper, now fitted for the very first time with the new full 2½-litre twin cam Coventry Climax racing engine.

In the words of Roy Salvadori (who finished second): 'With the new Climax engine, Jack Brabham and his Cooper had the edge on us. It was not by a lot, but it was enough. We could do nothing about him!'

Representative of the most modern front-engined Grand Prix cars in the World from both Britain and the Continent; yet now they were fast becoming no match for the new generation of rear-engined cars.

These classic front-engined cars were disappearing from the Grand Prix picture for ever.

Roy Salvadori in the new DBR4 Aston Martin.

Seen here really 'pushing it' in his Works Cooper during the '57 International Trophy is Jack Brabham, when his car, with the smaller engine, did not last the race. He had no such problems in the 1959 event with the full 2½-litres.

In that year he won not only the International Trophy, but, by the end of the year, became the first man to take the Driver's World Championship, driving a rear-engined car – the definitive shape of things to come!

Tony Brooks in the latest Dino Ferrari.

Photographic Notes

As mentioned in the introduction, in 1949 I bought a ZEISS IKOFLEX (6x6 cm), and the majority of the pictures in this book were taken on this camera.

A square format may seem a curious choice for a photographer who was out to take mainly action pictures, but a square gives the maximum area from any lens, and you can always 'crop' to the shape you wish in printing. Whilst it is obvious that the majority of motor-racing action pictures lend themselves to a horizontal format, there are occasions, particularly starts, when the extra depth of a square picture is well worth having. After all, if something is not on the negative, you can't have it in the picture!

The large frame-finder contained in the IKOFLEX viewing hood was ideal, and when trying to photograph in a dense crowd – the winner, for example – it was so useful to be able to hold the camera high above one's head, *upside down*, looking into the viewing screen, and shooting without obstruction.

The COMPUR-RAPID shutter on the 'IKO' wasn't bad, although the efficiency of such a between-lens shutter is not nearly as high as the focal plane type. I understand that a 1/500th setting only gives about a 1/380th – on a good day!

On occasions, I did dabble with other cameras: There was an EXAKTA, then a massive quarter plate GRAFLEX, on top of which I fitted a frame-finder. It worked after a fashion – but, oh the weight!

I also tried a Russian 35mm FED: their cheap copy of the LEICA, and, in the late Fifties, as a second string, I had a VOIGTLÄNDER RANGEFINDER-BESSA (6x9 cm.) Although the viewfinder was too small, I liked the large negative quality of the latter. But it was my old trusted IKOFLEX which I really loved, although with its visual film-counter one did have to work quickly.

For all my black-and-white racing photographs, I always stuck to Ilford film from the earliest days. The majority of pictures in this book were taken on HP3, and later I used HP4. The 400 ASA HP5 PLUS which I use today would have been great for shooting in really poor light, or the pouring rain, which some meetings in this country could attract!

Different circuits had their own particularly good, or not so good, photographic viewpoints, but I have always maintained that a bit of elevation was worth a great deal. This certainly applied at starts, when a bit of height would give much better separation of the cars. Goodwood was a case in point. I found that I could balance myself on the concrete guardrails, bracing my back against a Tannoy PA system stanchion, conveniently placed by the start line!

As a photographer, my motor-racing nostalgia also encompasses using the old cameras.

Nowadays, photographing with modern 35 mm equipment and zoom lens, etc. I never feel quite the same satisfaction from getting the picture I want with the help of a motor-drive that I had in the past when every shot counted.

There's a sneaking suspicion at the back of my mind that NOW I may be cheating a bit!